re•store (re•stor'), v.t. **1:** to put or bring back into existence or use   **2:** to put or bring back into an original state   **3:** to put or bring back into a former state.

Corvette Restoration

State of the Art

Published by

Michael Bruce Associates, Inc.

Corvette Restoration: State of the Art is published by Michael Bruce Associates, Inc. Printing by The Old Trail Printing Company, Columbus, Ohio. Binding by the Johnson and Hardin Company, Cincinnati, Ohio. Color separations by Engraving Arts, Dayton, Ohio. Typography by Spec-A-Type and Dwight Yaeger, Typographer, both of Columbus, Ohio. Photo/text credits, page 110.

Direct editorial correspondence to: Michael Bruce Associates, Inc., Post Office Box 396, Powell, Ohio 43065.

Second Printing

Book trade distribution by:

Motorbooks International
Publishers & Wholesalers Inc.
Osceola, Wisconsin 54020, USA ®

ISBN: 0-933534-14-0

Contents

Corvette Restoration

State of the Art

Restoration. To different people it means different things. As part of the auto enthusiast's vocabulary, it has always seemed to apply to antique cars. It inferred the resurrection of an unrecognizable pile of rusted junk to a dazzling showpiece too good to drive. It often required the fabrication of parts from scratch that had long been extinct. For a period of time -up to and including most of the sixties- the term definitely implied the renewal of something **old.**

Then things began to change. The change in attitude about a classic's age requirements coincided with what many auto enthusiasts perceived to be the constant degradation of new automobiles brought on by government meddling.

Whether that meddling was justifiable in the public interest or not is not the issue, but rather what government regulations did to the auto enthusiast hobby. The advent of stringent pollution control devices, and certain safety related requirements which resulted in increased weight, combined to drive performance levels downward relentlessly. One result of this was to make overnight "classics" of cars that were in some cases less than ten years old.

During the decade of the seventies, it is no secret that Detroit struggled to meet federal pollution standards at the expense of performance. Auto soothsayers, those amateur crystal-ball speculators who try to anticipate which cars will make them a bundle of money, came to the conclusion that cars which went very fast would appreciate very quickly.

Some have. But the assumption that performance alone creates a classic automobile is wrong. A classic is not created by later events. A classic is a classic the day it is built. It is a classic a year later, a decade later, a century later. It doesn't matter if it's a Corvette or a Barcelona chair.

Granted, Corvettes have been at the forefront of the pack. They've led the way in interest and in value appreciation. But the fact that certain Corvettes are blazing performers is only part of the reason. An automotive classic must be more. It must combine performance with style. It must be "right" in every respect.

Certain Corvettes are. Stand back and study the lines of a '63 coupe. It'll look just as good thirty years from now. Lift the hood of a '65 fuel injected roadster. Breathtaking. And it will go just as fast as that gorgeous engine would have you believe.

Despite the facts, there are still those who would argue that no Corvette can be a true automotive classic because no Corvette is old enough. Wrong.

The bulging hardware under the hood of a 1965 fuel injected Corvette creates doubt that the hood will even close. It will. And the engine will deliver as much performance as its appearance indicates. Fuel injected Corvettes were fast cars in an era of fast cars. In relative terms, even the base Corvettes of just a few years ago are fierce performers today.

This is not to say that just because something is a classic, everybody is going to be smart enough to recognize it from day one. The Corvette market is a good example. Corvettes built between 1953 and 1962 have always been viewed as collectible classics by those who loved them. And just about everyone recognized the '57 fuel injected model's potential from its introduction day. Chevy called it a classic in their 1957 ads. Saying it doesn't make it so . . . but in this case they were right.

The mid-year Sting Rays, those built between 1963 and 1967, were tremendous showroom successes and possibly the truest classic Corvettes that will ever be built. But not too many of us knew it at the time. We were spoiled by an era of great cars, the Jag XK-E, the Avanti, the Cobra. We were spoiled into thinking things would just keep getting better and go on forever.

The 1968 model Corvette suffered from what the public perceived as a drastic drop in quality levels which tainted the new models for years. In truth, the 1968 wasn't as bad as its reputa-

tion, and quality problems were under control by the time 1969 production began. But the stigma held on. 1974 marked something of a watershed year for the Corvette enthusiast because it was the last model year Corvette of the series not to be equipped with a catalytic converter, and the first to have soft bumper treatment at both ends. Neither of these items seem all that significant in themselves, but they just highlighted the fact that Corvettes were changing, in ways not considered positively by most enthusiasts.

Many sports car buffs came to the conclusion in the seventies that Chevrolet had already built the best Corvettes that they were ever going to build. Some felt that way in 1971 when engine compressions were reduced to permit the use of lower octane fuels. Some concluded that the 1972 model was the last good Corvette, since it was the last with chrome bumpers front and rear. Some thought it was 1973, and so it goes.

Whatever the reason or year, by 1975 an awful lot of people had concluded that some earlier Corvette model was the one they wanted. Since the 1953 through 1962 models already had their loyal but limited following, the effect was most pronounced on the 1963-1967 models. These were seen by many as the ideal Corvettes. They had great styling, more than adequate creature comforts, and blazing performance. They were modern classics.

In the meantime, something else happened to drive up the interest of first the 1962 and older models, then add to the fire building under the mid-year Sting Rays. In 1974, seven men founded the National Corvette Restorers Society. These seven pioneers, John Amgwert, Dick Campbell, Joe Chess, Tom Essig, Sam Folz, Jay Kellogg, Gary Mortimer, and soon after, Noland Adams, formed an organization dedicated to "the preservation, restoration, and enjoyment of early Corvettes." Within three years, membership exploded to several thousand, because the NCRS inception was perfectly timed to the explosion of public interest in restoring Corvettes. The NCRS initially limited its interests to only the solid axle Corvettes built during the 1953 through 1962 period, but later expanded its coverage to include up through the 1967 model.

Practically overnight the entire country seemed to become aware of the Corvette phenomenon, and interest blossomed everywhere. Corvette clubs that had been almost underground for years suddenly flourished. Publications sprung up to satisfy the thirst for Corvette information and entertainment. Concours events changed from local affairs where local folks steam-cleaned their engines and gave the exterior a fresh coat of wax, to major events of national prominence. The first Bloomington Corvette Corral in Illinois was held in 1973. By the 1975 gathering, attendance had grown to an astonishing 10,000. Bob McDorman Chevrolet in central Ohio sponsored its first Corvette concours in 1974. By 1976, it was awarding a brand new Corvette to the top concours entrant. Clearly, something very significant was happening in the Corvette enthusiast's hobby.

The surge in Corvette restoration interest paralleled the general interest in Corvettes and was a direct outgrowth of both the concours events and the desire to restore a Corvette that had the capability of being a more desirable automobile than a showroom example. Because of this, Corvette restoration changed from something people talked and dreamed about to something they actually undertook.

The Sting Ray models compare favorably to any high performance sportscar being manufactured today.

Restoring a Corvette is a unique activity, different in many ways from restoring an antique auto. This is because Corvettes are not ancient history. The oldest Corvette, the 1953, is a very modern automobile by most standards. And the Sting Ray models compare favorably in any measurable statistic to any high performance sports car being manufactured today, even the foreign exotics with price tags over the fifty thousand dollar mark.

Is this really true? Yes, it is. For example, the introduction a few years ago of the Porsche 928 was hailed as a milestone in high performance sports car production. Some auto magazine staffers picked it as the world's finest car, bar none. Nearly all magazines praised Porsche for its daring creation of an automotive engineering masterpiece, deservedly so. But for the sake of argument, let's see how a mid-year Corvette Sting Ray stacks up. Hold onto your seat, this may shock you.

Few organizations have had the profound effect upon a hobby as has the National Corvette Restorers Society. The NCRS first limited its interest to the "classic" Corvettes built between 1953 and 1962. But responding to enthusiasts, the NCRS later broadened its scope to include Corvettes built through and including the 1967 model.

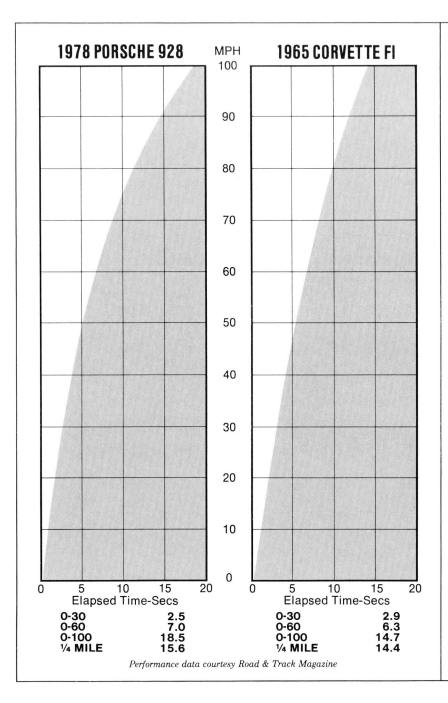

1978 PORSCHE 928		1965 CORVETTE FI	
0-30	2.5	0-30	2.9
0-60	7.0	0-60	6.3
0-100	18.5	0-100	14.7
¼ MILE	15.6	¼ MILE	14.4

Performance data courtesy Road & Track Magazine

Road & Track magazine tested a fuel-injected 1965 Corvette coupe in its December, 1964, issue. They tested a 1978 Porsche 928 fourteen years later in the April, 1978, issue. Comparisons like this can never be completely fair, but this one seems reasonable. The Corvette was fuel injected, so was the Porsche. The 928 had an extra gear in its five-speed manual, a slight advantage. This may be partially offset by the Corvette's lighter test weight of 3430 pounds compared to 3510 for the 928.

Listen to *Road & Track's* performance figures. Acceleration time from zero to sixty for the Corvette was 6.3 seconds and 7.0 for the 928. The spread became larger for zero to a hundred, 14.7 seconds for the Corvette and 18.5 for the 928. Top speed? Exactly the same at 138 mph!

Are the cars similar in size? The Corvette is a bit lower at 49.8 inches, the Porsche at 51.6. Headroom in the Corvette is better at 38″ compared to the 928's 36.5 inches. The cars are within a half-inch of each other in overall length.

We're not saying a '65 Corvette is a better car than a Porsche 928. Or are we?

1965 was the year of introduction for disc brakes for the Corvette and it will compare favorably in this category as well. Both cars utilize discs at all four wheels. The Corvette's system has 461 square inches of swept area, the 928 has 440.

We're not saying a '65 Corvette is a better car than a 928. Or are we? The point is that the measurable things are very close, often slightly in the Corvette's favor. Yes, the 928 is handcrafted and the workmanship is superb. It is also very, very expensive.

Is it any mystery why many enthusiasts have decided to restore a mid-year Corvette? The only mystery is that there are still people out there who've not fully awakened to the facts. The mid-year Corvettes are fabulous automobiles. Even equipped with base engines, they'll blow away 99 out of 100 cars on the road today. The writing is on the wall. Get one while you can.

The fiberglass body of the Corvette and the ease with which many parts can be obtained make Corvette restoration much easier and within both the technical and economic abilities of many more enthusiasts than the restoration of antique autos. Another factor is supply. There are very rare and unique Corvette models, but the overall supply of Corvettes for restoration is quite good in relative terms.

Some antique auto buffs still scoff at the use of the "restoration" term applied to Corvettes. This is something Corvette people will always have to endure. An argument can be made that what has been done to Corvettes in the past hasn't been genuine restoration. But what the antique guys call restoration is even less pure than what's been happening in the Corvette world. And we're getting better.

The history of Corvette restoration is an interesting study in evolution. At the time the Corvette was introduced in 1953, the typical automobile built in Detroit was viewed by the auto enthusiast of the era as being gaudy, overstyled, and above all, over-chromed. The rage in the fifties and early sixties was to "customize."

Now that could mean a lot of things, and certainly a lot of customs had little to brag about where the issue of clean styling was involved. But the good ones smoothed the bodies and stripped away excess chrome and created something that was cleaner and more eye pleasing than the original.

The first Corvettes certainly weren't gaudy or chrome-laden; in fact, their styling was a somewhat radical departure in this regard. But even the first Corvettes weren't immune to the customizer. If you're in your thirties, perhaps you remember the California customs from the likes of George Barris and others that appeared regularly at the local newsstand.

So in the loosest application of the restoration term, the early Corvettes often underwent a personalizing "restoration" that took them away from factory originality. In those days a bone stock Corvette was dull . . . you could get one anywhere. But a unique Corvette altered to your personal touch and taste, ah . . . that was something special.

The desire to personalize a Corvette continues today, but to a far lesser and non-permanent degree. Somewhere along the way, it became a mortal sin to "butcher" a Corvette away from its stock condition. This evolution gained the most steam in the early and mid-seventies when the mix of people searching for Corvettes tilted in favor of those who were buying the car purely on its own merits.

Each person's conception of what a stock Corvette is, or what restoration to factory specifications really means, varies greatly.

Call it enhancement,
improvement,
enrichment . . .
but don't call it restoration.

It is only recent history that a Corvette without additional chromed engine parts, and other cosmetic departures from factory originality, could actually win a major concours event. And even then, such cars typically had to be considerably better than anything that ever rolled out of the Corvette assembly plant at St. Louis in order to have a chance of winning.

This is a sad state of affairs. There's nothing wrong with someone making a Corvette better than it ever was, but this is **not** restoration. Call it enhancement, improvement, enrichment . . . but don't call it restoration. Our dictionary says restoration means putting back to a former, or original state. It doesn't say anything about making it better, or making it the way it should have been, or making it the way you'd have preferred it. Every definition of restoration you'll find translates to this when applied to Corvettes: **Make it like the factory made it . . . no better, no worse.**

The Corvette hobby now stands poised to enter a new era, the era of genuine restoration, restoration that takes a Corvette back to within a breath of the way it came off the assembly line. This is restoration done first and foremost for historical accuracy. The questions will never all be answered. All the arguments will never be resolved. The 100% correct restoration will never be achieved. But as more and more Corvettes are genuinely "restored," we'll get ever so close. It isn't for everybody, but is unquestionably correct. And it is unquestionably the coming state of the art.

Enter David Burroughs

The story of Dave Burroughs' early fascination with Corvettes is so very typical of many Corvette enthusiasts that in itself it is an explanation of the love and demand for these cars that has developed throughout the country.

Dave fell for the Corvette when the Sting Ray was introduced in 1963. He was in high school at the time and the Corvette could then be only a very elusive and unobtainable dream. 1965 through 1970 were college days at the University of Illinois, those times when hamburger money was hard enough to come by, let alone new Corvette funds.

Besides, Dave had become consumed in aviation and advertising, areas in which he now has dual degrees. The desire to own a mid-year Corvette never left; it just went on hold. Still, Dave made countless trips from 1963 through 1967 to a small dealer in Roanoke, Illinois. The dealer was Sam Leman Chevrolet, and Sam was big on Corvettes. Dave would go out on a Sunday afternoon when nobody was around, just to feast on the Corvettes' beauty. "Some day . . .," he thought.

Some day came in 1971 when Gary Steiner, the art director of the ad agency where Dave was employed, announced that he'd decided to sell his '67 Corvette coupe. The two men struck a deal consisting of Dave's '69 Cutlass and $300 cash for the silver Corvette.

For three years, the Corvette served Dave's every need. If business required a trip to Chicago, it was the Corvette that took him there. If a vacation to Mexico was in order, the Corvette dutifully and reliably accepted the challenge for Dave and his new bride, Carol.

As fate would have it, in 1973 Dave was living just around the corner from the site of the first annual Bloomington Corvette Corral, now one of the country's largest Corvette gatherings. Dave took a quick walk through that first day and thought, "Hey, this is pretty neat."

The next year, Dave cleaned up his Corvette and entered it in the Bloomington concours. In this first event he'd ever entered, he placed second in class, much better that he ever expected and by his own admission . . . more than he deserved. But the seed was planted, and in the 1974-1975 period Dave became very active in the National Council of Corvette Clubs, including being a co-founder of his local Corvette club.

He campaigned his '67 successfully, but by the end of 1975, he was being beaten consistently. It was a matter of his car's original and not perfect paint, and of the ever-increasing quality of competition. Well, in Dave's mind, this just wouldn't do. So he set out to restore his '67 into a Corvette that could win anything, anywhere.

By the terminology of the day, Dave's restoration was pure stock. There were no body modifications, no chrome where chrome didn't belong. But the car was over-restored to perfection. Lumps and bumps in the body were block sanded out. Door and hood fit and alignment were corrected to ideal. Every visible part of the car was repainted, polished, replaced, or replated to stunning brilliance. In 1976, this Corvette walked away with top in class at Bloomington, top in class at McDorman's, and top in class/co-best of show at the NCCC nationals in Orlando, Florida. It was the only Corvette ever to win what was then the big three, the triple crown, of Corvette concours competition. To top it off, Dave brought the car back to Bloomington the following spring and again took the class win, along with a grand championship in the **restored** category.

After that, Dave retired the '67, never to be seen again in concours competition. But something lingered. During the months he showed his car, Dave was told by admiring onlookers time and again how great it was to see a stock Corvette do so well for a change. Yet Dave knew in his heart that his Corvette may have been stock relative to the competition, but it was far from true factory originality in the purest sense of what restoration means.

By this time Dave was no longer working for the advertising agency, having accepted a position with an insurance company as its corporate research planner. Included in his umbrella of duties is that of strategic market planning. In a nutshell, a strategic planner's job is to conceptualize future trends and then to apply the knowledge of what is likely to happen to action plans for his company's near and long term projects.

Hardly a summer weekend passes that there isn't a Corvette show and swap meet held somewhere in the United States. The trend toward shows with a national significance started with the Bloomington, Illinois, Corvette Corral first held in 1973. Many reasons can be cited for its success, and for the success of several other annual national shows, but most important for Bloomington was the "swap meet" which permitted restorers to locate the components they needed.

It isn't surprising that Dave would apply the same forward thinking to the Corvette hobby. His conclusion was that Corvette restoration would move very sharply toward genuine factory originality and he wanted to be a part of it. This foresight, combined with his knowledge of showing Corvettes, led Dave to conceive the National Corvette Certification Board. Starting in 1978, Bloomington concours entrants were no longer competing against other entrants. Instead, each car was judged on its own merits and awarded gold, silver, or bronze certification (or none at all). It was conceivable to have all cars entered certified gold, or to have none at all in the gold category.

For the Certification Board, Dave put together a volunteer group of Corvette experts from around the country. To a man, the judges were proponents of the return to real factory originality. The whole idea of Bloomington shifted from a resentment-breeding competition between individuals and their Corvettes, to

a competition between each car and its hypothetical "zero mileage" twin as built by St. Louis. The purpose of the meet was to reward and acknowledge top calibre Corvettes, and to show owners of lesser cars how to elevate them to the gold status.

The radical departure of the Bloomington Certification Meet and its immediate popularity among enthusiasts convinced Dave that he was on the right track. Yet he soon came to realize that things had not progressed far enough. What the majority of Corvette people considered to be factory original was still considerably less. Dave also felt a certain pressure to practice what he preached. That is, since he was advocating strict factory originality, he felt an obligation to undertake a research and restoration project with high emphasis on **real** factory originality.

Dave shared his thoughts with a few other Corvette enthusiasts whose opinions he valued and found nearly total and enthusiastic agreement with his "back to factory" philosophy. One such enthusiast, Don Ellefsen, had already come to some of the same conclusions himself. Don and Dave found that their mutual feelings on the subject of authentic Corvette restoration were so intense and parallel that they decided to purchase and restore a car together. Since the project they envisioned was extensive and expensive, they thought they might as well plan on taking the finished car to McDorman's for a shot at winning a new Corvette.

But this thinking had to change. Dave's experience on the show circuit made him realize this new project had to be started with a specific goal in mind. They were either going to build a show winner, or they were going to restore a Corvette to factory originality. It was either or, but not both. If Jules Verne could somehow supply a time machine capable of plucking a '65 Corvette right off the final St. Louis assembly line and depositing it in the middle of a modern concours event, the sad truth is the car would not win. It wouldn't even place well. But it would be an historical masterpiece.

The more thought Dave and Don put into their choices, the easier the decision became. Given time and money, almost anyone can build a show winner. But only dedicated enthusiasts, willing to spend hundreds of hours researching, can genuinely restore a Corvette. The prospect of restoring a Corvette to as close to original factory condition as current knowledge and materials would permit . . . and the chance to be among the leaders in this sole purpose endeavor . . . excited both men beyond description.

The project that Dave Burroughs and Don Ellefsen undertook ultimately required over three years and four thousand man hours to complete. To our knowledge, nothing like it had ever been attempted before. Along the way, Don became the full owner of the car by agreement, with Dave providing the full restoration service for a fee. Dave will be offering similar services on a very select basis to other clients through Burroughs Enterprises in the near future.

To Dave's way of thinking, full service or turn-key service Corvette restoration is something that simply is not available anywhere today. To understand why he feels this way requires an understanding of what he means by turn-key services: Consulting. Research. Restoration. Packaging.

Without question, there are very knowledgeable Corvette people scattered around the United States, Canada, and even some foreign countries. There are enthusiasts with expertise honed so fine in a given area they can walk up to your Corvette and tell you a screw is wrong because the head diameter is a fraction of a millimeter too small. But all too often the people who know these minute details and trivia don't do restorations for themselves, let alone for others.

There are professional people who are very capable. There are paint specialists who can apply flawless finishes. There are engine pros who can put a Corvette powerplant right back to brand-new operating condition. There are trim shops that can make any interior look perfect. The problem is that these people tend to work alone and not to combine their talents with other specialists. The difficulty this poses for someone seeking a complete, high-calibre restoration, is obvious.

Compounding this, the specialists often have businesses to run and don't have time to research or keep up with the latest state-of-art restoration information.

Dave envisions acting as something of a bridge between those who know and those who do. He would use a combination of his own personal restoration techniques for some components and the services of the best labor specialists and best researchers, but

either way he would coordinate the client's entire project personally so that all restoration facets mesh with state-of-the-art research. Perhaps someday in the future he'll take the ultimate step and combine everything under the same roof.

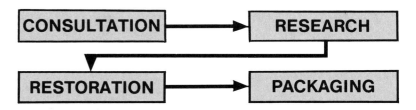

TURN KEY RESTORATION SERVICE

The Burroughs turn-key restoration service concept goes even beyond combining and coordinating services. What is completely missing from today's market is something Dave calls research and project consulting. Before a project begins, Dave would review all aspects of the restoration with a prospective client, putting special emphasis on cost forecasting. Sometimes a project may get no further than this first step if the projected cost is higher than the finished product would justify.

The consulting stage might also include purchase assistance. Dave would actually go with the buyer to help evaluate a car under consideration for purchase. This sort of assistance may or may not include a follow-up restoration of the car. Perhaps expert purchase advice is all the buyer is seeking.

If Dave did undertake the restoration, part of the turn-key service concept includes full documentation in tremendous detail. Not just a summary of what was done, but a complete record of the car before work commenced, the work performed, and the finished product. The media could be written text, photography, or video tape with sound track, or a combination of all three.

At the completion of the research and restoration stage of the project the owner would be treated to a multi-media presentation of every facet of the restoration his car underwent. The presentation would become the owner's property to go along with the car.

Then the car would be unveiled to him in an unforgettable ceremony. Packaging.

You can see what Dave Burroughs is aiming for. Even short of full restorations, we've all had those excruciating experiences of shoddy work, arguments about price, broken promises . . . things that can be so aggravating you just want to unload your Corvette and forget the whole thing. Dave's been through it and wants to save his clients the time and grief. He believes that whether someone uses his services, another's services, or undertakes the entire project himself, the results should be pure pleasure and satisfaction for the owner.

That's not to say there won't be some frustrations along the way. Another idea brewing in Dave's mind is to get the people who know together with those who want to know. He envisions professionally conducted seminars, possibly in conjunction with Corvette shows or other events. Try this for size. You sign up for a three day summer seminar to be held at a university campus. At 10 a.m. of the first day, you walk into room 202 for a lab demonstration of the latest fiberglass repair techniques given by someone who does it daily. After lunch, you proceed to room 210 for a presentation on the art of removing scratches from plexiglass, and the newest tricks for pulling and greasing rear wheel bearings. If you own a mid-year, you might want to catch the 4 p.m. demo on rebuilding electric headlight motors, but then again, maybe you'd prefer to see the latest techniques being used for refurbishing 1953-1955 seat frames being shown at the same time in another area. If Dave has his way, it'll all come to pass.

Hopefully when it does, most restorers will have set as their goal a final product that closely resembles their car's exact condition as it rolled out of final assembly in St. Louis. Restorations that have what Dave Burroughs and Don Ellefsen call the "natural factory look."

This does not simply mean that the correct parts will be on the car and they will be the right color. Natural factory look means that if several gradations of black were used, they will be reproduced in the same subtle gradations for the restored car. It means that if a part was sprayed such that another part nearby was sure to receive overspray, that part will be oversprayed again. It means that if a supplying vendor shipped parts to GM packed

loosely in boxes such that they incurred scratches, those components will be scratched in the same way for the restoration. It means that if a weird assembly procedure resulted in no paint behind certain screw heads where you would normally expect paint, the procedure will be duplicated faithfully. It means that if a particular chassis part is dipped in paint so that run marks and paint puddling were formed in predictable areas, the restored parts will have the same characteristics. It means that if a certain degree of orange peel could be found in all but special paint orders, and yours isn't one, then the orange peel will be put right back in. It means all this and much much more.

The Burroughs-Ellefsen restoration takes the term "original" and gives it a quantum shove several levels above where previous restorations have been.

It is important to understand the motives behind this restoration. It was built to show, but not to win show trophies. Think of it as a report. Think of it as being restored from the point of view of a researcher or journalist doing a report on a 1965 Chevrolet Corvette. As Dave Burroughs puts it, "It's no different than the reporter who's reporting the crash of the Hindenburg. The thing just fell out of the sky and burned up. The reporter didn't say, "Well folks, it's making a beautiful landing." Sorry, but that's just not what happened. Don and I just tried to do the same sort of honest reporting on this Corvette. If nobody does, nobody will know what they really looked like. The goal was not to make it any better than it was, or any worse. Flaws were not made just to make flaws. But if they were there, they went back in."

Dave is sensitive to and understanding of those who would view such a project with disdain, those who can't accept the idea of purposefully flawing a car in the interest of accuracy. After all, he's been on both sides of the issue. But the Burroughs-Ellefsen restoration is an extremely significant one. It is a harbinger of things to come. It serves several significant purposes. To those who would criticize, consider this:

(1) The car is an historical benchmark. It is not perfect, but it is as close as current knowledge and materials permit. As others pursue the same goals, even more knowledge will surface. Those who do follow in the same path will find they learn immeasurably more than if they just tear their car apart and refinish things to

make them look pretty from a cosmetic standpoint.

(2) The car is fascinating to look at and to scrutinize. There are far more subtleties than a typically restored car. It is especially entertaining to view if you understand the motives behind it.

(3) It is correct. It is wrong to flaw a car for no reason, or to do a sloppy restoration, but if it was characteristic of factory originality, it is correct.

But it is not 100% correct. The concept and goals were, but anyone who understands what restoration means, understands that no restoration can be completely correct. The important thing is the direction this restoration has taken and how it will influence the Corvette hobby in the future. As more of these restorations are done, more truths will evolve.

There will be controversy. But instead of worrying about who's picked the pebbles out of their tire treads more diligently, the discussions will center on what the factory did and didn't do. Restorations, judging, and values will shift to objectivity rather than subjectivity as factory originality becomes the final arbiter. More than anything else, the prestige of owning an older Corvette will magnify. In a very positive way, it will eventually be we Corvette people who look down our noses at the rest of the auto enthusiasts in humorous disdain as they struggle to play catch-up in the restoration state-of-the-art.

The Car

The Corvette selected for this restoration was serial number 194675S114971, a Nassau Blue 1965 convertible equipped with the 396 cubic inch, 425 horsepower engine. It was well equipped with such extras as leather interior, power windows, telescopic steering, teak wheel, gold line tires on knock-off wheels, and four-speed transmission. All the options were properly documented with GM paperwork that was still with the car.

Before any work was started, and continuing throughout the restoration, every effort was made to establish as much of the car's identity and history as possible. Dave Burroughs and Don Ellefsen purchased the car from Mike Hanson, a noted Corvette restorer in the Chicago area. Mike had purchased it from a gentle-man named Steve Dangremond on the West Coast. Mike Hanson considered restoring the car when he bought it, but it hadn't been touched when Don and Dave acquired it. Copies of past title work showed that Steve Dangremond had gotten the car from one H.C. Schneider of San Francisco. But that is where the history stopped.

The last address Dave had for Mr. Schneider was several years old. Sure enough, when Dave tried to phone, the information operator indicated that she had no record for anyone of that name. Dave wrote several letters to Mr. Schneider at the last known address hoping than one would get forwarded. They were all returned as undeliverable.

This might have seemed like a good place to give up, but Dave persisted. He considered it vital to trace this Corvette back to its original delivery in 1965. After all, a great deal of time and money was being invested in its restoration and it seemed a shame not to have the full historical background to tie the package together.

Besides, there were some very practical reasons for contacting all the previous owners. Each and every Corvette seems to leave the assembly plant with a personal identity all its own. Each will have some little idiosyncrasy, some unique characteristic. When viewing a Corvette fifteen years later, a restorer will note certain things he just doesn't understand, things that don't make sense. Perhaps a little part isn't just like the other similar models he's viewed over the years. Did the factory do it differently on this particular car for some reason? Did the dealer change it? Did an owner change it? Without being able to talk it over with all previous owners, you can never be sure. There will be loose ends. And there were just such loose ends with the '65 in question, things Dave couldn't understand. So despite the dead end, he was determined to find the mysterious H.C. Schneider.

In February of 1979, Dave went to California on business. While there, he tried again to contact Schneider by phone. There was no listing in the San Francisco phonebook, nor in any for surrounding areas. He called all the Schneiders listed anyway, hoping that one might be a relative. Nothing.

Dave continued the search. He went personally to the last address he had for Schneider, figuring that maybe the new residents remembered Schneider or where he'd gone.

Henry C. Schneider
President

Mr. Dave Burroughs
Bloomington, Illinois 61761   May 15, 1980

Dear Dave:

   Glad to hear the restoration of my 1965 Corvette is coming along so well. I'm
attaching a picture that was taken just after I returned from picking up the car in
Detroit...must have been sometime in late July or early August, 1965.

   I drove it directly from Detroit to Muscatine, Iowa, skirting the Chicago area,
and from there a direct line across southern Iowa to Omaha to Salt Lake City to Reno
to San Francisco to Palo Alto, California, my home at the time.

   I had trouble with the temperature running hot and had been warned that this
engine was usually in the 240° range. However, when I got to Reno some kid in a
service station noticed that the tubing had been reversed. To further expand this,
the tube running from the radiator to the aluminum expansion tank on the right side
had been installed so as to enter where the overflow tube should have been connected. After the drive from Reno, Nevada, to Palo Alto, re-examined and it was
quite obvious that it had been connected wrong. I changed it and after that had
almost no problem with over-heating and/or loss of radiator coolant.

   You also mentioned the heat riser. No, there was no wrapping on this tube. Just
a stainless steel tube running from the right side manifold to the carburetor.

   As to the chrome housing on the electronic distributor, I did not enlarge or
change position of the cutout. Incidentally, when I sold the car with approximately
80,000 miles of driving, these were the original brake pads. I did have to replace
the calipers on one wheel due to the parts just wearing out. I did replace the
radiator with a copper one only because I felt that the aluminum would be wearing
out. It hadn't and I saved it, but made the change due to driving in the California
valley in high temperatures. This necessitated some cutting of the molding holding
the radiator as the copper was apparently a half inch or so higher.

   I would appreciate getting this picture back, Dave, and keep in mind my proposed
trip to New York. I'll be very interested also in seeing the book you're working
on devoted to this restoration. It gave me many, many hours of pleasant driving
and it will probably be the only "memorable" car that I will ever own.

Cordially,

Henry C. Schneider
President

HCS:my

*Locating a Corvette's previous owners can be difficult, but the
results are often worth the effort. Not only is the car's history
documented, but a previous owner may be able to shed some light on
details that explain unique characteristics, information that could later
prove invaluable in a state-of-the-art restoration. Such was the case
when Dave Burroughs located Henry Schneider, as indicated by Mr.
Schneider's letter to Dave.*

The folks at the address had never heard of Schneider, but they rented the property and suggested Dave contact the owner in the hope that she might remember something. Dave reached the landlady, and she did remember Mr. and Mrs. Schneider. But she had no idea where they'd gone. Could she remember anything about them that might help? Yes, she did seem to recall that Mrs. Schneider worked for one of the airlines, perhaps United.

Finally, a ray of hope. Dave contacted personnel relations at United and after several telephone transfers and waits, Mrs. Schneider was on the line! Yes, her husband had owned a blue Corvette. Yes, she was sure he'd be delighted to learn that the car was being restored to new condition. Yes, he would most certainly be pleased to assist in any way he could. The car had been very special to both of them.

The mysterious H.C. Schneider turned out to be Harry C. Schneider, president of a company now located in Hawaii. He was indeed delighted to assist in the restoration, and he was a knowledgeable auto buff who understood what Dave was trying to accomplish. And his memory of the car and its characteristics proved to be excellent.

One of the great pleasures of the Corvette hobby is the new acquaintances that result, and this was just one example of how that can happen. Beyond the enhancement of the project itself that resulted from locating Schneider, which was significant, Dave had developed a new Corvette telephone friendship.

The information which Harry Schneider was able to furnish filled in the missing gaps in the history of number 194675S114971, and also cleared up the mysteries that Dave had uncovered about this particular car. An idea of the sort of information that a previous owner can provide is best exemplified by one of the letters Harry sent to Dave, which is reproduced in this text. This is one of several letters and many phone calls, but it nicely conveys some of the pleasure a past owner can receive from the knowledge that something once very special to him is being so beautifully restored and preserved. Harry Schneider said it best in his final sentence, "It gave me many, many hours of pleasant driving, and it will probably be the only "memorable" car that I will ever own."

Ah, sweet inspiration.

Stage One: Preparation

Cost Analysis

A Corvette restoration is not something a person just dives into one sunny weekend. At least it shouldn't be. It should be very well thought out in advance. Two of the more important considerations are the car that is to be restored and the degree of restoration to be undertaken.

In almost every case, the cost of a Corvette restoration will be more than a person doing it for the first time could possibly imagine. For this reason, it is important that the Corvette's value after restoration be taken into consideration before the project begins. A careful study may reveal that the degree of work planned is not justified by the car's likely value potential. It could also work in the reverse, but this is not the more common mistake made. A discussion of cost analysis principles is necessary to get the problem under control.

The essence of the problem is that it's easy to spend an amount that when added to the original cost of the Corvette would equal a figure that the car will not come close to being worth when the work is finished. Huh?

Say for example the cost of the restoration you plan, excluding the cost of the car, is $10,000. Surely, it would make more sense to spend $9000 for a car to restore that would be worth $20,000 when restored, than to spend $6000 for one that might not be worth $12,000 no matter how well restored.

The numbers used in the example are unimportant, but the concept is. It is a mistake that has been made many times. The Corvette's tremendous appreciation over the years has made it a winning investment for many people. But just because you've heard the great stories of how much somebody has made, don't believe for a moment that it's impossible to lose money with an older Corvette. It's possible. Not every Corvette turns out to be a financial winner. We hear the success stories, but the disasters get swept under the rug. Maybe it's the embarrassment.

A point could be made that this is just a hobby and the dollars do not matter. You may want a perfect example of a model Corvette that you loved when you were younger and couldn't afford. Now you can, and you don't care what it costs. If you're in that position, great. But it still wouldn't hurt to know how things stack up before you begin.

This business of how extensively to restore a Corvette can be backed into from two approaches. First, let's assume an individual already owns the car and he is determined that it's the one he's going to restore. If cost is a consideration, then he has to tailor the type of restoration to the car he already owns. The second approach is where the person has decided on what type of restoration he wants, then goes searching for the appropriate Corvette. Either approach is fine and the goal for each is the same. The degree of restoration should match the car being restored.

There's more to consider. How will the car be used? Is it going to be a flawless show piece, never to be driven? Is it going to be an historical report like Dave Burroughs'? Or is it to be a car to be driven and enjoyed everyday? You can see that each direction will require restorations quite different in scope . . . and cost.

Back to the subject of value for a moment. The restoration equation is simple, $A + B = C$. "A" is how much the unrestored car cost or is currently worth. "B" is the cost of a restoration. "C" is the total of the two. We consider the restoration equation before we begin any work because if cost is a factor, we don't want "C" to be more than the car is worth in the restored state.

How do we determine what a specific restored Corvette model will be worth one, two, or three years from now? Is there a handy little book we can just look the figures up in? No. There are various price guides around that purport to do the job, but they do not. They cannot.

They cannot for two reasons. First, the market changes. Just because some type of Corvette has been "hot" the past two years and has gained some percentage increase in value, you cannot comfortably predict that the same thing will happen in the next two year period. At the same time, some sleepers will emerge and increase dramatically.

The second reason is that even if you eliminate the future trends aspect and try to just establish current market value, that's

THE RESTORATION COST EQUATION
A + B = C

A *is the cost of the Corvette or its present value*
B *is the cost of the restoration*
C *is the total of A and B or the total invested*

also impossible to do with accuracy by looking at someone's published figures. This is because of the difference in conditions and especially because of the way different people perceive quality. So often terms like "mint," "completely restored," "100% original," and "all numbers match," are used in advertising Corvettes by people who don't have the faintest notion of what they really mean.

The books that have attempted to present guidelines for old car values try to accommodate the differences in condition by attaching some sort of qualifying numbers. A five might mean a so-called "100 point" restoration, whereas a one might be a basket case. The numbers in between represent the degrees of condition between the two extremes. It doesn't take much imagination to realize that it's tough enough to get two people to agree on the condition rating a car should have, especially if one of the two is an owner and the other is a buyer. Add to that the factor of a very

fluid market, a fact of life for the Corvette world, and you realize that such value guides are doing well if they're within 50% of a Corvette's true value.

Factor in others' opinions, what you read, and your own gut instincts based on following the market as best you can, then make your own prediction. You won't be exact, but hopefully you'll be close. Having arrived at the guess yourself, you'll understand where the error came from.

How do you "keep up with the market?" People who buy and sell Corvettes often are quite current on what's selling and for how much. If you know someone like that, tap him for information. There are excellent monthly Corvette publications that specialize in used Corvettes and parts, such as *Vette Vues*, and such a publication can be an excellent source of information. *Vette Vues* usually has over a hundred used Corvettes advertised by private owners in each issue. Occasionally someone will go back through publications like these and average the asking prices for different Corvette model years over a several year period to show the relative increase in prices. Of course "asking" price is one thing and selling price is another, but such a study has so many hundreds of inputs that it is statistically of value, certainly at least in relative terms.

Once you're comfortable with the value you've attached to the car you have or want to buy to restore, you must predict its value in the future after varying degrees of restoration.

The biggest single determinant of a Corvette's value in the past has been scarcity. In the 1953 introduction year, Chevrolet built a mere three hundred Corvettes. The following year, nearly four thousand were made. Would you expect that the '53 model, despite the fact that it looked almost exactly like the '54, would be far more valuable because of the lower number built? Of course. Would you anticipate that the five Corvette Grand Sports, specially hand built models fabricated by Chevrolet Engineering under the supervision of Zora Duntov to be Cobra-eaters on the racetrack, would be a bit expensive today? You'd better believe it.

For the regular production models, enthusiasts have historically preferred those that could be considered milestones. This usually means the first and sometimes last of a body series, but mechanical breakthroughs may alter that formula.

It wasn't the fastest Corvette ever, but it was the first, and only 300 were made. It takes a sharp eye to tell a '53 from a '54, of which 3640 were built. But the scarcity of the '53 puts it in a value category all by itself.

The 1956 and 1957 Corvettes had almost duplicate bodies. There were 4467 Corvettes built in the 1956 model year and almost half again as many, 6339, the following year. But the 1957 has always been more positively viewed by collectors because of the mechanical breakthroughs of four-speed transmission and fuel injection availability.

All of the 1953 through 1962 models have a strong and loyal following, but another year that stands out is the 1962 model. In the first twenty-five years of Corvette production, the most dramatic design change was made between 1962 and 1963. With the exception of the engines and drivetrains, the two models were totally different. For the person who likes the "old" style Corvette, those with solid rear axles, exterior-opening trunks, and high, "arm out the window" driving position, the '62 is the ultimate. It has the extra power of the famous 327 cubic inch engine line-up used in Corvettes from 1962 through 1968, yet it has all the features of the classic Corvettes that some enthusiasts prefer.

The 1963 through 1967 series Corvettes are the models that really set the Corvette movement on fire and these are often the

ones which command the highest values. There are exceptions, of course, but many enthusiasts view these cars as the premier models of the Corvette's first quarter century. Their arguments are strong indeed.

The chassis that Zora Duntov put under the first Sting Ray in 1963 served the Corvette just fine in almost unaltered form right up into the eighties. In time, horsepower went down and weight went up, which makes the mid-year Sting Rays just that much more desirable because when they were built, performance and styling were everything. Uncle Sam's regulations were just starting to arrive when the '67 model was being built and the effect was minimal. The teakwood steering wheel and three-prong spinners on hubcaps and aluminum wheels were gone due to safety considerations, but that was about it. The engines were fire-breathers and continued basically unmolested through 1970.

The first and last of the series guideline would seem to dictate that the 1963 and 1967 models are the ones to own. They have indeed shown tremendous increases in value and popularity. The 1963 is the first and in coupe form, the only Sting Ray with the dumb but beloved split rear window. Dumb because the split created a blind spot big enough to hide a Peterbilt. Beloved because GM knew it was dumb and took it out after only one year. Presto! First of the series model year and a unique feature. Besides, the split did look great from **outside** the car!

1967 is the last of the series, a car that Corvette history tells us was not even supposed to be built. The car that appeared in 1968 was originally scheduled for 1967 introduction, but was deemed too wild for public consumption. It was "toned" down (mainly by lowering outrageously high fender peaks) and delayed by a year. At the last minute, designers did a restyle of the '66 by just removing trim, adding some interior and exterior refinements and the cleanest Sting Ray of all was hatched. The car that shouldn't have been wound up being one of the greatest.

But other mid-years are very much in demand. The '65 saw the introduction of four-wheel disc brakes to the Corvette, removing the last legitimate gripe the always negative car magazine guys could muster. 1965 was also the last of the Duntov-Dolza fuel injected Corvettes. This meant that it was the only year that the Corvette's original fuel injection system would be on cars with

TOWARD AN AMERICAN CLASSIC . . . THE 1957 CORVETTE
WITH FUEL INJECTION! It is with considerable pride that
Chevrolet invites you to examine an engineering advance of great significance, available
on the 1957 Corvette. It is fuel injection, and in the Corvette V8 it permits a level of
efficiency hitherto unrealized in any American production car: *one horsepower for every
cubic inch of displacement . . . 283 h.p.!* In addition, there is unprecedented responsiveness, even during warm-up: virtually instantaneous acceleration and significant gains
in overall gas economy.

This is another major step in the creation of a proud new kind of car for America:
a *genuine* sports car, as certified by its record in competition. But a *unique* sports car
in its combination of moderate price, luxurious equipment and low-cost maintenance
with fiery performance, polo-pony responsiveness and granite stability on curves.

It is our intention to make of the Corvette a classic car, one of those rare and happy
milestones in the history of automotive design. We take pleasure in inviting you to
drive the 1957 version—and see just how close we have come to the target. . . . *Chevrolet
Division of General Motors, Detroit 2, Michigan.*

SPECIFICATIONS: . . .

CORVETTE
by Chevrolet

*Advertising something as a "classic" is usually the best way to insure it
won't be, but not so in the case of the 1957 Corvette. Chevy said "It is
our intention to make of the Corvette a classic car, one of those rare
and happy milestones in the history of automotive design." Without
question, they did just that.*

brakes to match. For what it's worth, Zora Arkus-Duntov says
this is the all-time ultimate Corvette. He should know.

There were many other desirable treats sprinkled throughout
the mid-year Sting Ray production run. Air conditioning, leather
interiors, 36 gallon fuel tanks, aluminum knock-off wheels, AM-
FM radios, and the Z-06 performance package all made their
Corvette debuts during the 1963 model year. The fuel injection
system left in 1965 and the 396 cubic inch "big block" arrived. So
did the teakwood steering wheel, goldwall tires and side exhausts.
The big block became 427 cubic inches in 1966, and the following
year the limited quantity, ultra-high horsepower engine was
ushered in by way of the L-88. In 1967, only twenty were built.

That's just a brief sampling of what took place during the mid-
year Sting Ray era. There was never a period in Corvette history
when so much happened in just five years. The range of purposes
that a Corvette could serve was broad. A Corvette could be
ordered with base engine, automatic, and air conditioning. Combine those with a tall 3.08:1 road gear and you had the ultimate
cross country touring machine. Go the opposite direction with
high performance engine and low gearing, and you could rule the
city on Saturday night.

There's no mystery about why the mid-year Sting Rays are
popular. They had it all. We knew it when they were built, and
time has just proved it all that much more. If you're of the philosophy that what goes up must come down, and you're waiting for
the prices of these cars to drop so you can buy one, you're only
fooling yourself. Prices of some may have leveled, and some
other years may well catch on. But these mid-years will only
increase in value as time rolls on. The elements are too simple.
The supply is limited and the demand is tremendous. The supply
won't grow, the demand will. And at the bottom of all this is the
undeniable fact that they were just plain fabulous automobiles.

There is still a bit of residual snobbery some folks hold toward
Corvettes. Those mega-buck people who always thought of Corvettes as being a little juvenile. But even those folks are coming
around to the facts of the matter. And when they finally and
completely come to grips with what these cars really are, look
out. Value-wise, you're going to see the mid-year Sting Rays
become the modern day Duesenbergs.

What does Dave Burroughs think about all this? Dave likes the 1965 and 1967 models. He likes a lot of the others too, but these are his favorites and he believes that there is so much to learn that it is best to limit one's interests. He very much admires all of the other mid-year Sting Rays but admits that his expertise of the others is limited. The only way to know a '65 and '67 the way he does now is to disassemble a few. The '65 and '67 models are the only two he's personally torn into, and the only two he plans to, except maybe the '66. By the way, he has nothing at all against '66 Corvettes, but thinks they're a bit less interesting because everything seemed to happen the year before and the year after.

Dave doesn't care for high option Corvettes. He sees the Corvette as a performance machine. Options that sap power like air conditioning and power steering don't make sense to him. He views others like vinyl covered hardtops, teak wheels, and power windows as unnecessary frills. To him the best Corvette is one with high performance options and aluminum wheels (because of their lighter weight) and not much else. But he stresses that this is personal preference, not advice. Highly optioned Corvettes have been excellent investments in the past and many will certainly continue to be.

Remember the restoration equation mentioned earlier? It was stated as $A + B = C$ where "A" is how much the unrestored car cost or is currently worth, "B" is the cost of the restoration, and "C" is just the total of the two. Once you've gotten a handle on what it is you want to restore and what it might be worth when you're finished, you have an idea of how large "C" should or shouldn't be. Now it's time to put a price tag on the cost of the restoration itself. Lets call this the restoration cost analysis.

If you thought figuring out what your car was going to be worth someday in the future was tricky, get ready for bad news. Determining how much the restoration will cost is even tougher. Dave Burroughs says this is one of the most difficult aspects of a restoration with regard to accuracy. This is especially true for someone going into it for the first time. Example: If you go to a restoration shop and ask what something will cost, the answer might be "time and materials." That's called a blank check. On the other hand, if an estimate can be obtained, the quality of work expected and that being quoted might be entirely different. There's always a tendency in all of us to respond to a quote with an offer of price compromise. That usually means quality compromise too. For someone comtemplating a restoration for the first time, the attempt to predict the cost to be incurred can be maddening. But it's absolutely essential to try. By comparing actual expenditures to estimated, a tremendous education will be gained (inflicted?) on the restorer.

A few years ago, costing a planned restoration wasn't such a big deal. You got a paint job estimate and steam cleaned the engine. But that wasn't a restoration, it was a cosmetic refurbishing. Nothing wrong with that, and probably there are many Corvettes around today that deserve or need no more.

But a restoration is much more. In the most current meaning of the word, a restoration takes a Corvette back to the day it was completed on the assembly line. Done correctly, that could mean restoring, but not necessarily replacing virtually every piece of the car, every body, chassis, interior, and engine component. No wonder that trying to figure out with some accuracy how much all this is going to cost can be mind boggling.

Ah, but there is a bright side. As more and more restorations are being done, more and more information is becoming available. This book is a prime example. While it is true that every restoration is unique, no book has ever presented one in more detail. By scrutinizing the logic and steps that Dave followed in this milestone event, the intent is to give the reader the tools necessary to more accurately assess his own project before even turning a wrench. The intent goes beyond that, of course, but this is one of the most important.

The Burroughs-Ellefsen restoration story is not meant to intimidate anyone. Its purpose is to encourage, not discourage. Restoring a Corvette is not as difficult a task as some would have you believe. GM engineers didn't design the Corvette to be easy to restore later, but that's exactly the way it turned out. The Corvette has a fiberglass body that never rusts. The fiberglass body unbolts from the metal chassis intact. What more could we ask for?

Unfortunately, one thing this text cannot do is tell you how much **your** restoration will cost. You'll have to estimate that yourself. But Dave Burroughs can offer some guidelines and advice.

According to Dave, the least expensive restoration is sometimes the one that results in the best looking car. How can that be? It goes back again to the intent of the restoration and how you define "best looking." If your intent is to have a pretty car, but you could care less about factory originality, you can minimize or eliminate a considerable amount of expense. Dave spent hours on the phone tracking down exactly the right types of paints. If you figure flat black is flat black, you can buy all you need at the local

GM engineers didn't design the Corvette to be easy to restore later. But that's exactly the way it turned out.

hardware. If you want exactly the same black that GM used, and you want it on the right parts, you'll incur some expense in locating it. Likewise, you'll incur transportation expense in actually getting it. The categories of transportation, telephone, research and documentation expenses (see chart) accounted for 14% of the Burroughs-Ellefsen restoration cost.

Another item often overlooked is interest expense. If you borrow the money to do your project, the interest costs are obvious. But if you dip into your own cash reserves, you should consider what you lost by not having the money available for something else. Your local rate for liquid investments is as good a guide as any.

The other items shown on the restoration cost percentage chart are the ones you'd expect to find, though the proportions may surprise you. Don't forget these proportions are different for every Corvette restored. If you have a car with a very sweet engine but a terrible body, the percentages will skew accordingly.

Also affecting such an analysis is what work is done by the restorer and what is sub-contracted to others. The chart does not include any cost input for Dave's time. Since the body and paint, engine, and interior areas had considerable outside costs involved, these are quite high.

Restorers assume before starting that their main cost centers are going to be paint, new interior, and engine. That's usually

WHERE THE MONEY GOES

EXPENSE BREAKDOWN FOR THE BURROUGHS-ELLEFSEN RESTORATION

1. Included within Parts: • Interior 12%
   • Body 8% • Engine Accessories 4% • Chassis 12%

2. Research includes telephone, photography, mail

3. Engine Rebuild includes labor and internal engine parts

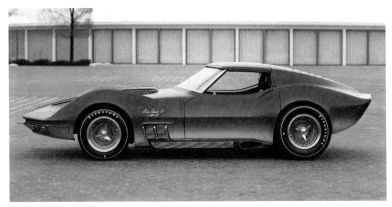

Above: In 1965 and 1966, the auto world awaited another all-new Corvette body design for the 1967 model patterned after this Mako Shark II dream car. The projections were right, but at the last minute top GM management stepped in at the urging of Zora Arkus-Duntov and postponed the introduction until 1968 so that the extremely high front fender peaks could be re-designed.
Below: The 1968 model had to be better than the "mid-year" Sting Rays that preceded it to fill expectations, but that was a mighty tall order. The new body, a first attempt at removable roof panels in a coupe version, and a stepped-up production schedule all combined to create a low quality image that hung for years, lighting a demand fire under the previous Corvette models that continues to this day.

correct and it holds true for the Burroughs-Ellefsen project. But study the chart carefully and you'll see the main pitfall restorers meet. They accurately determine the "big three" costs, then throw in a few bucks allowance for the rest. In the Burroughs-Ellefsen project, the big three together accounted for just 43% of the final total. This is exactly how a restorer can wind up spending double his projection despite decent estimates for body/paint, interior, and engine. Watch out.

One last comment regarding cost analysis. Don't be shy about seeking help. Not too many people document things as thoroughly as Dave Burroughs, but often you can piece together quite a bit of information from different sources. Be as thorough as you can and keep all the calculations you make at the start of the project. Check yourself as the project moves along. No well-run business operates without knowing where its money is being spent. An individual's restoration is not a business, it's a hobby. But it's a hobby that can turn very sour if its a financial disaster. Don't subscribe to the theory that playing accountant takes the fun out of a restoration. The truth is just the opposite.

The Sequence Plan

After the cost analysis is made, the feasibility of the restoration justified, and the degree of restoration decided, the next step is **not** to start tearing the car apart. It's an easy mistake to make, but it would definitely be a mistake.

That next step is the making of a restoration sequence plan. The plan of a precise, detail-oriented person will reflect those traits, but even if you don't think of yourself as precise or a master of detail, the restoration plan is something you must not avoid. Why? Because a good restoration plan will minimize wasted time. You may have time to burn, but wasting it is aggravating and discouraging. It takes much of the pleasure and satisfaction out of the project.

A restoration plan is a sequencing tool. The idea is to spend whatever time is necessary to study your Corvette and what you're going to do. Spend hours, days, weeks, whatever it takes to determine what you're going to do, **and** in what sequence.

This sounds elementary, but it isn't. You'd be surprised how many first time restorers blow this step completely. Restorations that aren't sequenced properly can drag out forever. Next time you see one of those Corvette-for-sale ads with the line ''80% restored, lost interest,'' you can bet your torque wrench the guy didn't understand sequencing.

Take the simple example of plated parts. It's pretty obvious that if you take a bucket of 20 parts to your plater to be done at one time the cost is going to be less than if you make twenty trips with one part each time. It sounds awfully basic to say, ''Take all your parts needing plating in at the same time.'' But most restorers don't.

Most restorers take things in batches. Maybe the body will be attacked first and all the bumpers, emblems, and exterior trim make the trip. Next the restorer digs into the engine compartment and discovers there are a few things in there that require plating. Another trip. Next comes the interior, and more items go to the plater.

How much simpler to spend the time at the outset determining what parts need plating and what type of plating. Get all the parts together and make one or two trips to the plater for the whole project. Schedule it properly and all the parts will be back on your shelf ready when you need them. Your plater will be happy (they hate the ''Jeeze, I forgot one'' customer), your cost will be minimized, and your time maximized.

A number of variables affect a sequence plan. They include the degree of restoration, what work will be done by the restorer and what will be farmed out, the budget, readily available manpower, and the previous experience of the restorer.

Under the category of degree of restoration comes the decision of whether the restoration is to be a body-off type. If it is, there are critical sequencing decisions to be made. An ''I'll cross that bridge when I come to it'' is asking for trouble in any restoration. It's big trouble if it's a body-off the frame type.

To understand the potential problems, we should review how GM put the Corvette together in the first place. A Corvette first starts to look like a car when the chassis comes down the assembly line to take on sub-component assemblies. One of these is the engine itself which was assembled and painted at another location and shipped to the Corvette assembly plant where its accessories, hoses, shielding, and other items were added before it was lowered into the chassis. The body was an assembled unit, painted and almost complete, when it met up with the chassis.

Everybody agrees that the best restorations are those which duplicate as close as possible the way GM originally assembled the Corvette. If you're doing all the work yourself, or all the work is being done on your premises, you can just about do it. You can rebuild and refinish the engine isolated from the chassis. You can refinish the body isolated from the chassis. All the chassis work can be done isolated from the engine and body. Then everything can be mated back together almost exactly the way GM did it. If there is paint overspray, the overspray will be where it belongs.

But it may not be possible. Say you are not equipped to handle the fiberglass repairs and painting in your facility. If you pull the body and start working on the chassis, how do you get the isolated body to the second location? Putting it on a flat-bed truck is possible, but not very practical. Bringing it back that way in a finished condition is even worse.

There are a number of options open if all the work is not to be done on the restorer's premises. Dave Burroughs faced this problem, made a decision which worked out alright, but is doing it differently for his next restorations. What he did and what he does now will both be covered in the story which follows. For now, suffice to say that you must sequence the movement of the three major components in a body-off-the-frame restoration. The components are chassis (less engine), engine, and body. You may need to sub-divide the components further. If the frame is to be sandblasted or chemically stripped of rust, plan its movement into the sequence. You can sequence a restoration plan right down to a daily schedule, but if that's not your bag, do carefully sequence the movement of the major components, those that don't move so easily, before you start. It's a time investment that'll repay itself many times over.

Stage Two: Disassembly

Documentation

Now that a cost analysis and a sequence plan have been developed, it would appear that the time has come to begin the restoration. True enough, but the next step of the actual restoration process is not just twisting wrenches. The next step is one called documentation.

Documentation to most enthusiasts means paperwork. It would include the original window sticker, invoices, registrations, repair receipts, correspondence between owners, anything that helps to document the history of the car being restored. These are all examples of documentation and they all contribute to establishing a car's authenticity and value.

True documentation means even more and restoring a Corvette properly presents you with the opportunity to document your Corvette to the ultimate degree. This is because you can add to the car's history the story of its rebirth. Surprisingly, the most important documentation will occur as you disassemble the car. It will be during this stage that the Corvette will bare its soul to you, but you must be attentive to the clues and messages that lie hidden under years of dirt, grease and grime. If you take your car apart with no more on your mind than remembering which parts go where, you've just eliminated the most interesting phase of a restoration. If you don't accept that, then at the least you've missed the chance to make your final product much more valuable to a future buyer.

The time to start documenting your restoration is before any part is removed. The documentation will continue through disassembly and reassembly. This is because some things cannot be documented after disassembly, but others must be.

Documentation should be done through a verbal/written, and visual technique. The verbal/written can be accomplished through the usual note-taking process, or you may wish to record your comments and observations on tape as you see them. The visual part usually means photography. It also includes illustrations and more exotic techniques of movie or video tape.

Dave Burroughs employs all of these techniques with emphasis on photography and video tape. His video tape presentation includes his voice dubbed in to correspond to the visual image. Granted, Dave's intent went beyond what one would expect. He

You can over-restore a Corvette.
You can't over-document it.

knew that he'd use the documentation material later for instruction purposes. Still, there is absolutely no such thing as over-documentation. You can over-restore a Corvette. You can't over-document it.

It is very sad that so many Corvette restorations, certainly the majority, have been done with an almost total disregard for documentation. It's almost as though the cars lose their individual and unique identities. A restoration may create a show piece, but in the process the character of what GM produced in St. Louis has been sacrificed. This need not be the case, regardless of the type of restoration.

Some would argue that a Corvette being restored for show need not be documented . . . that's it's only important for a "natural factory look" project. Not true.

Think a few years into the future when you're showing your car to someone, a prospective buyer or just an interested enthusiast. He may be viewing something very attractive, but he has no way

DATE 197_	RECORDING TACH TIME	TODAYS FLIGHT	TOTAL TIME IN SERVICE	DESCRIPTION OF INSPECTIONS, TESTS, REPAIRS AND ALTERATIONS — ENTRIES MUST BE ENDORSED WITH NAME, RATING AND CERTIFICATE NUMBER OF MECHANIC OR REPAIR FACILITY. (SEE BACK PAGES FOR OTHER SPECIFIC ENTRIES.)
9-27	.3		.3	Adjusted Timing & Carburation
9-28	.4		.7	Runs @ 30-70 MPH OAT 70° Temp 210° Press 45# 20A
9-29	1.5		2.2	Runs 1-55 Loop (BT ST TO ST) OAT 70° Temp 215° 45#
	1.5		3.7	155 Loop Danvers Road Course 3500 RPM 210° 45-50# ①
10-3	.6		4.3	Danvers Road Course 4000 RPM/4th Gear OAT 65° 210° 45#
10-5	.9		5.2	2 Round Robin Danvers OAT 55° 190° 45# 5 AMPS (Replaced #2 Boggs/Slry/STD)
				① See Photo/Slide

DATE 197_	RECORDING TACH TIME	TODAYS FLIGHT	TOTAL TIME IN SERVICE	DESCRIPTION OF INSPECTIONS, TESTS, REPAIRS AND ALTERATIONS — ENTRIES MUST BE ENDORSED WITH NAME, RATING AND CERTIFICATE NUMBER OF MECHANIC OR REPAIR FACILITY. (SEE BACK PAGES FOR OTHER SPECIFIC ENTRIES.)
10-11	.3		5.5	Idle Round the Block OAT 60°/180° 45# Finger Starts
10-12	.5		6.0	Road Driving Carb Problems/Stalls OAT 50°/180° 45-50#
10-27	1.0		7.0	Hudson-Carlisle-Return Up/Down Shifts 2500-3500 RPM / Dificlt to Start/Hot or End of Test Poor Idle/Dies
10-28	.5		7.5	Exhausted Choke units Idle OK Finger starts ok
10-30	.3		7.8	Autocross School 3000 RPM Finger Start OAT 40°/180° 45#

Dave Burrough's interest in aviation served him well throughout his Corvette restoration. This is a sample of the data log kept for the engine every time it was started. While it is possible to "over restore" a Corvette, there is no such thing as too much documentation.

of knowing the car's true background. Was this an excellent original just freshened up? Was it six wrecks, maybe not even of the same year, pieced together? Given no documentation, some people will assume the worst. Imagine the frustration you'll feel if you've done everything correctly, but can't convince anyone of it.

Now imagine the response you'll receive if you couple a very beautiful Corvette with a 300 slide presentation of it before, during and after restoration. Anyone with any sense will conclude you're the type of person who does things correctly, and that trait would certainly carry over to the restoration itself.

Documentation results in much more than just a record as to the conscientiousness of the restorer. It records exactly what the car was before restoration began. Add that to whatever paperwork was available and you've got a car with no mysteries.

A valid excuse for not documenting a Corvette restoration would be that the restorer has something to hide. But you certainly can't conclude that there's anything wrong with a car that's been restored but not completely documented.

In the past, documentation hasn't been viewed by most restorers as being very important. The emphasis has been on the result, not with what it was or how it got there. It is exactly for this reason that the very high value Corvettes are now unrestored originals. If you watch the market, you realize that the genuinely untouched car, even one whose overall condition is a bit run down, has been commanding the highest prices. The reason is simply that there aren't that many around. People contemplating a restoration would much rather see what they're getting. People just buying a car to drive now with a future restoration years off feel the same way. Too many Corvettes have been restored improperly, or modified to suit someone's personal tastes. Don't make the same mistakes.

Exactly what should be documented? Detailed answers to that question will emerge as the coverage of the Burroughs-Ellefsen restoration continues. But in general, you should plan your documentation to describe the components on your car and their condition, how they are assembled, and in what sequence they are assembled. It isn't always possible to achieve all of these objectives, but if you attack each area with them in mind, you'll be on the right track.

Keep this caution in mind. Few of us who restore Corvettes are also professional photographers. Some restorers try to overcome that problem by hiring someone for the task. The results are often unsatisfactory.

Zero in on the tiny numbers,
the gas filter, the overspray patterns . . .

First, most professional photographers are not professional auto restoration photographers. It might take them as long to master the craft as it would you.

Secondly, there is a logistics problem. You can bring in a pro to photograph the car before you start and after you finish. But a lot of documentation occurs between those events. If you call in the pro everytime you find something interesting during disassembly, you'll run up a fortune in photo bills and waste time in the process. What most often happens in these professional photographer deals is that many important shots just aren't taken.

Your best bet is to master adequate photographic skills to do the job yourself. There's nothing that says you can't hire the best pro in town after you're finished to shoot some spectacular shots you can blow up to poster size for your office or den. But plan on doing the nitty-gritty work yourself. If you're mechanically inclined to the extent that you're willing to tackle a restoration project, you can handle the photography as well.

One last photographic caution. The human eye is a miraculous tool that can absorb a great deal very quickly. Amateur photographers make the mistake of assuming a camera can do the same. It can't. It must be aimed at precisely what is to be shown, and it must be close enough to show the detail desired. Remember that your eyes are seeing the subject full size. When you view the finished photograph, your eyes will be viewing the same scene, but reduced to a small print or even smaller slide. Don't try to show too much in your photos. You can take shots of the complete chassis, but get in close for the details, too. Zero in on the tiny serial numbers, the gas filter, the overspray paint patterns. In a properly done restoration, remember there is no such thing as too much photography, nor too much documentation.

Staging

There is one other concept you should be familiar with before starting to disassemble your Corvette. It's called staging. Even though it's a simple concept, it's another of the critical planning steps that many restorers ignore.

Here's how staging works. During disassembly, parts are grouped according to the type of cleaning required. Cleaning can range from a mild soap and water scrub to sandblasting. In between those extremes are such things as enamel reducers, lacquer thinners, paint strippers, and chemical acid baths. Don't confuse cleaning with restoration. If a part needs restoration, that comes later. Cleaning a part with soap and water is not restoration and neither is cleaning it by sandblasting.

Having read the previous paragraph, you may be saying to yourself, ''Big deal, that's obvious.'' It seems obvious, but the typical restorer doesn't practice staging effectively. The reason is that there's a tendency in everyone to do one area at a time. Interior parts get put in one pile, body parts in another, and chassis parts in several more. The restorer works on one pile until he finishes it, then attacks the next. The mistake he is making is to group the parts by their function or location, rather than by what cleaning they require.

If staging is done correctly, the parts will be grouped by what they need, not what they are or where they came from. You may have instruments grouped with chassis and engine parts. The idea is that when you stand up to the sink to wash parts, you do them all at the same time. When you set up your lacquer thinner bath, you do it just once. Working on groups of parts in this manner saves enormous time.

Nobody is smart enough to stage with 100% effectiveness. A complete Corvette restoration involves thousands of parts. Even with the best laid staging plans, a few parts will be missed. Something that looked like it would clean up with soap and water will require lacquer thinner. Something that looked like it would clean up with stripper will need sandblasting. Some parts will just be overlooked. These are lousy excuses for not bothering to stage at all, especially if in your haste to see progress you realize you've just sandblasted away forever the hidden secrets in code markings of your Corvette's unique history that could easily have been cleaned with soap and water and preserved indefinitely. Ignore staging and the previously discussed sequencing in your restoration plan, and you might just see a one year project stretch out to five. Or worse yet, leave clues to your Corvette's history in a sandpit. Don't laugh, both happen. What happens more often is "lost interest" and no completion at all.

If cleaning finishes a part so that it requires nothing further, it can then be regrouped according to area, such as interior. If further attention is required, then the part gets grouped with parts that need similar attention. There'll be a group of parts that go to the plater. Many parts will require painting, and they'll be grouped separately depending on the type of paint and the application method. Some parts will have to be repaired, perhaps by straightening or welding. Electrical items like headlight motors, alternator, starter, radio, and gauges may have to be rebuilt.

One part could make all the piles. Cleaning might reveal that it has a crack that requires welding. The welding may distort it so that it has to be straightened. Then it may go to the plating or painting group. But eventually it and all parts wind up in their respective area groups. You can see that ignoring staging and doing each part on an individual basis could literally take forever.

The cleaning stage of a restoration is inexpensive in real dollars, and inexpensive in time outlay if staged properly. In fact, it can sometimes save replacement part dollars when you discover that a terrible-looking part cleans up beautifully. For this reason, cleaning should be sequenced in before the restorer commits to the high dollar outlays such as new interior components. Often the cleaning stage is required before you can get a handle on which components need restoration and which need replacement. Planned properly, the high dollar items come into the picture just after you've finished component restoration. Everything will be on hand and everything will have been cleaned, restored, or replaced. If cash flow isn't considered in this way, some of the expensive items will be laying around gathering dust while other components are still being restored.

Dave Burroughs is a well organized individual and he sequenced and staged his restoration very tightly. It still took over three years and several thousand hours. Don't be discouraged. Phased into the Burroughs-Ellefsen restoration was a great deal of research. There were countless phone calls and trips to view other cars. A beautifully restored Corvette was only half of this restoration's goal. The other was the learning experience.

Throughout the restoration, Dave did things over and over until he was satisfied. Putting the engine in and out of a test car five times is one example of his persistence to approach perfection. If he couldn't figure out what kind of paint was used on a chassis part and how it was applied, the project went on hold until he found out. It might require a visit to the factory, a call to the vendor that supplied GM, or a study of one of the handful of very low mileage '65 Corvettes still left. If every effort yielded nothing, Dave had to use his best judgement. Then if the answer turned up later, the part was redone. It is important to understand the thought behind this restoration to comprehend the time involved. Dave Burroughs is his own most demanding critic. The chassis components were stripped and painted, then stripped and painted two more times in efforts to duplicate factory gloss, texture, and patterns. The frame itself went through eight different paintings, five to experiment with finish, three to experiment with application techniques.

At this point in the restoration, Dave interrupted the work to take the chassis on tour, including the big show in Knoxville in early 1980. The idea of this was to expose as many people as possible to the work already done and see what could be learned. Loading the chassis in and out of a trailer created some wear and tear, so it was taken apart one more time and refinished again to factory freshness.

These things happened not just because of what Dave Burroughs was striving for, but also because he was doing many things that just hadn't been done before. Thanks to him, many of us will not have to pay the same price.

Once the cleaning stage was completed, Dave Burroughs broke the actual restoration into four phases. They are body, chassis, engine, and interior. It's well to think in terms of these four major parts groups in all your pre-planning. You may wish to group the interior with the body in planning your disassembly routine though. That's the way this text will attack it.

Body Disassembly

Personal preference and the logistics of where work will be done and who will do it should all influence a restorer planning the disassembly sequence for his Corvette. A good rule of thumb is to get anything perishable out and away from the car first. If your Corvette is a convertible, start with the hard and soft tops. Then go to the interior. You certainly don't want the misfortune of slipping into a seat with a screwdriver in your back pocket, or grease on your heel.

Remove the interior components carefully and store them away from your worksite in a clean, dry location. At this stage of your restoration, do not throw anything away, even things you're planning to replace.

For instance, if you will eventually purchase new carpeting, having your old carpets to refer to will not only aid in installation, but will enable you to determine if your new carpet is properly made before you install it. If it turns out the new carpet is molded or cut incorrectly, you have your old carpet to prove it to the manufacturer. Plus, if you had to install the new carpet in order to find out it was trimmed wrong, the source is going to be very reluctant to take it back.

It doesn't sound fair, but it is fact. If you can take the new carpet back with no glue on it and show the source it is incorrect compared to the originals, your chances for an adjustment are good.

Another reason for keeping original interior parts is that you may want to salvage something you hadn't planned on. Using carpet as an example again, you may find that the only new carpeting available for your model year does not have the correct heel pad, or uses a different style welting around the edges. Possibly the originals can be stitched in even though the carpet itself is shot. This sort of preciseness might not be appealing at the start, but it will be after a few hundred hours have been invested. There is such a vast array of reproduction materials available to the Corvette enthusiast that it becomes easy to throw things away in the belief that a new or repro duplicate can be purchased. Some

Corvette parts are not available anywhere. Some of those that are, are terribly far from being acceptable duplicates.

There aren't many trade secrets involved in removing interior parts since most unscrew or unbolt. A few words of caution are in order for the carpet removal, however. Do not just grab one end of the carpet and give it a jerk. It will come out if you jerk hard enough, but the jute backing will be ruined in the process. The jute is that junky-looking fiber material between the carpet and the fiberglass floor. Unless your Corvette has been a chronic leaker, the jute should be reuseable. It's a great idea to at least try to salvage it because it fits the contour of the floor so well. It's had many years to get comfortable down there. If you replace carpet and jute, you'll have a difficult time smoothing out the bumps. Neither the carpet nor jute pads will fit exactly properly and replacing both just doubles the trouble.

Remove the carpet and jute carefully, easing it up very slowly. You can pull the jute and carpet as a unit and separate them later, or pull the carpet out first, then the jute. The second technique

---

Assume you're going to use every part, even though you plan not to.

---

takes longer but works better. Either way, you'll need a putty knife or single-edge razor blade or whatever you find in the shop to help the glued surfaces separate.

Use a cautious, deliberate technique of disassembly throughout this entire state, not just for carpet removal. Assume you're going to reuse every part, even though you plan not to. Emblems and trim might not be considered perishable, but get them off the car and safely stored in the early stages also. Use whatever system of cataloging parts that's comfortable, but remember that what looks very obvious during disassembly may not be so obvious a year or so later when you put it back. Just throwing everything into a big box in the corner of the garage is asking for disaster.

Once you have the interior out, you can turn your attention to the exterior. Most restorers remove "hard trim" from the body such as bumpers, door handles, trim, and glass. They then pull the body from the chassis. Dave's restoration called for a diffe-

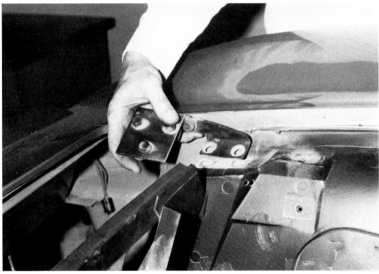

The key to a successful state-of-the-art restoration lies as much in the disassembly stage as in restoring or assembling. Carefully observe every part as it is removed. Is it plated? Is there overspray on it? Is there paint behind it? What conclusions can you reach? Are these conclusions consistent with the factory assembly manual, or with other similar Corvette models that you've observed?

rent sequence plan. He pulled the engine out of the car before the body was removed. The engine was to get a professional rebuild and Dave wanted to give Jim Otto, the "pro" he'd entrusted the engine work to, plenty of time. Also, Dave prefers to pull the engine first so that it's not in place when the body is removed. This makes the body easier to remove since it doesn't have to be lifted as high. Besides, Dave has pulled engines out of Corvettes so many times, he has it down to a science, a science we'll review later in this text.

There are other advantages to pulling the engine before the body. Less the engine weight, a Corvette can be rolled around the shop manually with ease. Plus, Dave wanted all body work done while the body was on the chassis, and he wanted it done before the chassis was restored.

Dave's shop is not equipped for painting a complete body and he doesn't care to work with fiberglass, so he entrusted both of these activities to Royal Coach in suburban Chicago. Not doing everything on site brings up the question of who does what and where. And how do things get moved around?

Dave made a sequencing decision regarding the body that he's since decided could be improved on. The decision was to do all body repair work first, while the body was still on the chassis. The repaired areas, not extensive on this car, were finished down and primed but no finish color was applied. The body was then pulled from the chassis and put aside for two years while research and chassis work continued. After the chassis was just about complete, Dave wrapped it in Saran™ wrap and gently put the body back on. The chassis was thus acting as a platform on which to move the body back to Royal Coach for finish painting. The purpose of the wrap job was to prevent paint overspray from hitting chassis parts. The chassis and body are not mated when painted at GM, so other than a factory repair there's no way that body color should wind up on chassis components.

When all body work was finished, Dave was able to trim the Saran™ wrap completely away without disturbing anything. Even so, Dave now feels it is better to do all body and paint work first, including finish painting, before the body is ever lifted from the chassis. This is how Dave does his restorations now and this is what he recommends to any restorer who cannot do everything on site. Each technique has its advantages and disadvantages, and both suffer from the fact that neither is precisely the way GM did it in the first place.

Despite the negatives, Dave concludes that doing all body repair and finish painting before the body is removed is the best choice for the restorer who cannot do all work on site.

The technique that was used on the featured '65 Corvette, that of doing body work before the body pull and finish painting much later, has the advantage of allowing a long time lapse between the fiberglass repairs and the application of color coats. This is desirable from the standpoint of permitting the fiberglass to "do its thing." It can shrink, expand, warp . . . whatever it cares to do. If several months elapse between the repairs and the final finishing and color coats, chances are good the body will be stable and paint cracking later due to shifting fiberglass will be minimized.

A caution to be kept in mind is that fiberglass curing virtually ceases at low temperatures. If yours is a winter project, the body should be stored where there is heat at least part of the time. Several months of cold temperatures may equal only a few days of warmer temperatures. How warm? The warmer the temperature, the faster the cure. Most fiberglass is compounded to work best at room temperature and that means about 70°.

The second technique, that of doing all the body work including finish painting before the body is pulled, eliminates the need to elaborately protect the chassis from overspray. What's wrong with this technique? First, if adequate time is allowed for the fiberglass repairs to cure, the body-chassis combination is going to be out of your shop for quite awhile. If you're doing your own engine, you can be working on it in the interim, but if it has been sent out also, you may be without much to do for a long period. Maybe that fits your schedule fine, but think it through carefully.

The biggest drawback of all is the old overspray nemesis again. Granted, you may be overspraying a chassis that will be completely redone anyway. But you might in the process foul up the upcoming chassis documentation stage. You might cover up some interesting tidbits, or at the least create confusion regarding which overspray belongs and which does not. If the car has been repainted already, this consideration doesn't mean much.

Another potential problem is that the finished body will be stored in your shop while chassis work is done. There's always the chance that something will happen to damage it.

A final drawback is the cash flow. Body refinishing is always a major expense in any restoration. By doing it all early, you've encountered a heavy cash outlay far in advance of the project's completion.

Despite the negatives, Dave concludes that the technique of doing all body repair and finish painting before the body is removed is the best choice for the restorer who cannot do all work on site. He feels that the overspray problem can be minimized with careful masking, and that a trace of overspray on a frame that's to be refinished anyway is preferable to body-color overspray on a restored frame.

You'll make your own decision based on your own capabilities, schedule, and the car you're restoring. If fiberglass repairs are extensive, you will lean to the first technique to build in as much curing time as possible. If repairs are minimal, you may lean to the second, especially if you place less emphasis on chassis documentation, or if your chassis is badly rusted and overspraying it is no great sin. Adequate care with either technique will produce perfectly acceptable results.

Regardless of the sequence you select (and there are more possibilities than those just discussed), you should plan to do fiberglass repairs while the body is bolted to the chassis. Some very good restorers get very good results with the body off the chassis, but the risks are greater. Even though it's to be pulled later, a body still bolted to the chassis is in the position it will be spending most of its life. If you attempt to clean up a door fit (Dave doesn't improve panel fits in a natural factory look restoration) with the body off the chassis, you'll probably find the fit will change again when back on the chassis. Maybe it was all right in the first place! Also, a body off the chassis is more difficult to work with. It flexes, it moves around. Bolted to the chassis, it's a heavy, stable platform that stays put.

You must plan to support the body adequately when off the chassis. Tales have circulated about restorations of early Corvettes where the body literally broke apart in the middle when supported only in the middle with the door open or off. This is a might extreme and unlikely, but inadequate support can certainly create uneven stresses that cause problems. The '63 through '67 coupes and all late model "T" tops are the ones you can worry about least. They are structurally very sound and you can expect little trouble with them although extra caution doesn't hurt.

All pre-1963 models and all later convertibles are another matter. In Dave's case, no extreme precautions were taken because all actual work on the body (other than some under-body cleanup) was done when the body was on the chassis.

But a problem can occur if you insist on working on the body off the frame with the doors open. To insure that no undue stresses are induced, you must support the body evenly in the front, center, and rear sections. If you support the body at the same locations it was bolted to the chassis, you have nothing to fear by opening the doors. If you're not confident about your support mechanism, you could remove the doors before the body is pulled off, and bolt in a support bracket between the front door hinge and rear striker locations.

Dave Burroughs doesn't like the idea of a support bracket, nor does he agree with removing the doors to spray them. Removing them for repairs to the hinges, or just prepping them, is fine. But GM painted the doors when they were on the car and that's the way he feels it should be done in a correct restoration. Gleaming, flawless door jambs and spotless hinge pockets may impress a concours judge, but they're a dead giveaway that the car isn't an original. They didn't leave St. Louis that way, and Dave strongly feels they shouldn't be restored that way either.

As a matter of fact, Dave not only didn't remove the doors, he didn't restore the jambs at all. As he saw it, the paint on the inner doors and jambs was just as it was when it left the factory and there was no reason to refinish. Dave followed two simple rules throughout this restoration: If something didn't need restoration and was factory original, leave it alone. If something did need restoration or wasn't factory original, restore it to factory specs as close as possible.

Some of this doesn't set well with all restorers. Some want to see perfection when a door is opened. Well, the owner is the one who'll have to live with what is done, so if that's what he wants, so be it.

If you do choose to remove the doors, here's another caution to bear in mind. Do not spray the finish color coat on the doors or any other body parts (other than convertible hardtop and rear filler panel) separately from the body. Spraying parts separately creates paint match problems. Even spraying from the same paint mix, you'll likely find that doors sprayed separately from the body look like they don't match. This is especially true for metallic paints. It occurs because it is very difficult to keep the metallic content consistent throughout application. It won't be noticeable unless there is an abrupt change, which is exactly what can happen if you spray the body, then move over later and spray the doors while they're leaned against the work bench.

You've seen this paint mis-match on cars driving down the street. A repainted off-color door sticks out like a sore thumb. You'll notice it most on a high metallic color like silver or silver-blue. You'll notice it least on a metallic if it's dark, like the dark blue introduced on the '63 Corvettes. The problem is practically non-existent with a non-metallic, provided your paint mix is consistent and you rub out all texture.

Ah, but you don't want all texture out in a natural factory look restoration. This is another area that the Burroughs-Ellefsen restoration differs from others. Factory paint application wasn't mirror perfect. Minor orange peel and texture in paint was common and in predictable areas. After lengthy and explicit instructions from Dave, Royal Coach faithfully duplicated these paint imperfections in his restoration.

The argument against duplicating factory paint flaws is that maybe GM painted a few perfectly, say a Corvette that was walked down the line for a GM executive. If you can document that your Corvette received special attention, you certainly have every right to duplicate that attention. It just so happens that the '65 Dave restored **was** a walk-through, a car documented as being built for GM promotion purposes. Despite that, its paint was characteristic of production Corvettes built throughout 1965, flaws and all.

The Body Pull

With the possible exception of an engine tear-down, no part of a do-it-yourself first time restoration is more frightening than pulling the body off the chassis. Sure enough, without the proper precautions, it can indeed turn into a disaster. With the proper precautions, there is little to fear. And being able to work on the chassis with the body off, having easy access to all those components you normally have to lay on your back to reach . . . dirt dropping in your eyes all the while, is such a gratifying treat that the time and effort of pulling the body will be very well spent.

At this stage, the body should be nothing more than a shell. The interior, trim, and glass will all have been removed. It's at this point that you'll start to appreciate how nice it was of GM to make the Corvette the way they did. The body and chassis are separate assemblies, joined together as one of the last operations at the assembly plant. Years later, here you are able to reverse the process for disassembly, then almost duplicate it in re-assembly. The body and chassis are not locked together by a zillion spot welds as in "unibody" construction. The Corvette body is **bolted** on. Unbolt it, get a few interference items out of the way, and it just lifts off. Wonderful.

There are some precautions. You must plan ahead and build some type of holding mechanism for the body while it is off the chassis. Some people just set it on the floor, but that leaves a lot to be desired. The ultimate is a jig on wheels that supports the body in approximately the same locations as it was bolted to the chassis. Some restorers even bolt it to the jig. Even if you don't intend to do much work on the body while it's off the chassis, the ability to roll it around the shop comes in handy.

Dave Burroughs had a convenient corner of his garage where the body could be stored safely and not disturbed. Since his plan called for virtually all body work to be done with the body on the chassis, he did not invest in the time and expense of a moveable jig. Instead, he built a fixed support out of concrete blocks and stud lumber. The lumber supported the body at the locations it bolted to the chassis, including a frontal support that reached up and held the radiator support.

Above: Dimensional variances between a Corvette body and chassis are compensated for by shims, nothing more than slotted spacers.
Below: The restorer has the choice of replacing each shim exactly where it came from, or making a list of the quantity used at each body mount. Rarely is more than one thickness of shim used. Dave Burroughs preferred to replace each shim in its original location so he made a rigid chassis diagram and taped the shims to the diagram as shown.

Some people in the business of restoring Corvettes have elaborate hoist mechanisms set up for lifting the body. Most of us won't be doing this more than a few times, so the simple and effective technique is manpower. Eight men of average strength can handle a Corvette body without strain. Some restorers use only six, but the extra two add a safety factor, especially nice if the body has to be held suspended for a while for some unforeseen reason.

In addition to the eight people actually lifting the body from the chassis, have some extra people on the scene. Call them troubleshooters and shim spotters. Troubleshooters to look for trouble. Shim spotters to spot shims.

Spot shims? Yes, and according to Dave Burroughs, this is one of the most important aspects of a successful body pull. To understand why, a brief review of the body drop technique used by GM to assemble the Corvette is in order.

St. Louis is often referred to as the place where Corvettes are made. A more correct statement would be that Corvettes are assembled in St. Louis (and now Bowling Green, Kentucky). In truth, Corvettes are "made" all over the country. That is, the parts are made all over the country and not all of them by General Motors. The parts come together at the assembly plant.

Anyone involved in manufacturing knows what the word "tolerance" means. No manufactured part can be consistently made exactly the same. Engineers establish a tolerance range into which parts must fall to be acceptable. There is a perfect size, and there are sizes that are all right provided they're within a plus and minus range. The tolerance range in some industries such as aircraft and aerospace is very small. In the auto industry, they're considerably larger.

In the case of the Corvette, virtually every part in the chassis and body has a tolerance range when it is built. Obviously then, no two chassis are exactly the same, and no two bodies are exactly the same. How then does GM compensate for a body that doesn't quite fit a chassis? The magic little critter that saves the day is called a shim.

A shim is nothing more than a spacer. During assembly, shims are placed between the Corvette body and chassis to compensate for variances due to tolerance ranges. What happens is that the body tolerance is accepted, but the chassis is corrected. Before a

body is mated to a chassis, a special apparatus (in essence a dimensionally perfect body) is temporarily dropped onto each chassis. The apparatus tells the operator how many shims are required at each body mount location to true the chassis to a perfect body. The operator marks a code (more on this later) on the chassis to indicate the correct shim placements. Of course, the actual body that the chassis later receives will not be perfect, but it will be within what GM considers an acceptable tolerance range when mated to a dimensionally corrected chassis.

If GM didn't go through this procedure for the Corvette, the tolerance difference between the chassis and the body could be

---

If GM didn't go through this procedure, the tolerance difference between the chassis and body could be sufficient to crack the body when it's bolted down.

---

sufficient to crack the body when it is bolted down. Or worse, it could put the body in a bind that causes it to stress and crack later after it's sold. Not the righteous path to customer satisfaction.

What all this means to the restorer is this: You must be extremely careful to shim each body mount location as it was originally done by the factory. The shims were temporarily held in place at the factory by a paper-type tape (usually tan, sometimes black). When a restorer pulls a Corvette body, what's left of the tape may hold the shims in place. Or the shims may fall to the ground. Or they may stick to the body and fall to the ground later as the body is being moved to its holding device.

This is where the shim spotter comes in. As the body is removed from the chassis, the shim spotter watches for falling shims. He (she?) picks them up and places them on the ground near their proper frame mount location. As the body is lifted, the spotter checks each mount location on the body to be sure no shim is stuck to it. If some are stuck, they're removed and placed where they belong on the ground. It doesn't hurt to have a couple of people doing this, perhaps one on each side of the car.

Any number of techniques can be used to catalog the shims to make sure they get back to their proper body mount when the body and chassis are eventually mated. There are only a few different shim thicknesses used, and often you'll find that all shims on a particular car are the same thickness. But there may be two at one body mount, none at another, five at yet another. If the shims are the same thickness, it isn't critical that each be placed in the exact location it came from, so many restorers just make a chart showing how many shims are required at each location. Dave preferred to put each shim right back where it came from, so he constructed a little rigid chassis diagram and taped the shims onto the diagram in the correct locations.

Here's an interesting sidelight and caution regarding body shims. If you are planning a frame replacement, consider the hazards involved. Remember that the purpose of the shims is to dimensionally correct the chassis, not the body. Some restorers not aware of this have simply replaced the rusted frame under their good body and used the same shims they found when the good body was lifted off the rusted chassis.

They got it backwards. They should have used the shims that were with the good frame, which were probably long gone. Using the wrong shims could magnify a tolerance difference and cause real trouble. You'd be better off using no shims at all if you have no idea which are correct. The odds are you could get away with this, and many restorers have. Considering the thousands of Corvettes built, if GM forgot about the shim procedure they'd have hundreds of cracked bodies to contend with. But the majority would be ok.

What this boils down to is that you the restorer shouldn't take the risk. If you're spending thousands of dollars and many hours, you don't need stress cracks in the finished product due to improper shim placement. If your car has already seen a body-off, convince yourself that the guy who did it knew what he was doing. If you're considering a frame replacement, try to get one with original shims still in place. If you can't, take it to a good frame specialist for a dimension check so that you can at least shim in the right direction. The best situation is to be restoring a car with a salvageable frame (many of the rustouts are rusted only in localized areas and can be repaired) that has never been separated from the body. If that's the case, you need only get the shims back where they came from and you're in business.

Chassis Disassembly

Now that the body has been removed from the chassis and is safely out of the way, chassis disassembly can begin.

From the very start of this restoration, Dave Burroughs and Don Ellefsen looked at it as more than just the creation of a pretty car. For Dave especially, it was to be an education in how GM built a '65 Corvette. Anyone who thinks there's nothing to learn during disassembly is wrong. The opposite is true. This is where you'll learn the most, if you proceed correctly. The important thing is not to plunge in too quickly. Don't make the mistake of tearing everything apart and shipping it to the sandblaster or stripper. Study everything carefully before and during disassembly. Constantly ask yourself, "Why did they do it that way?" Even if your chassis is rusty, don't assume it doesn't have some interesting stories to tell you.

The chassis of Dave's restoration '65 did look rusty and dirty, but it turned out to be in excellent condition. Dave made a practice of starting cleanup with a mild solution of soapy water and soft brushes. This removed the dirt and some of the scum that looked like rust but wasn't. This light cleaning technique allowed much of the frame's original coating to show through. More than that, it allowed coding marks to show through. For instance, there was a white stenciled part number along the side frame rail. Before removing it, Dave found stencils that matched perfectly, then made a reference chart so that these and other numbers could be duplicated later in appearance and location. He even went so far as to let the stencil slip to duplicate the sloppiness of the original.

Another hand written number was found on the side frame rail. On Dave's '65 this number was "4-9-65," most likely the date the frame was pulled from inventory or put into production, since the final completion date for the car was April 12, 1965. This makes sense since the date is upsidedown when viewed now, so the frame was upsidedown when the number was written.

To be able to duplicate this number later after frame refinishing, Dave made a guide by holding a clear piece of plastic sheet over the numbers and tracing them onto the plastic, Later, he'd use

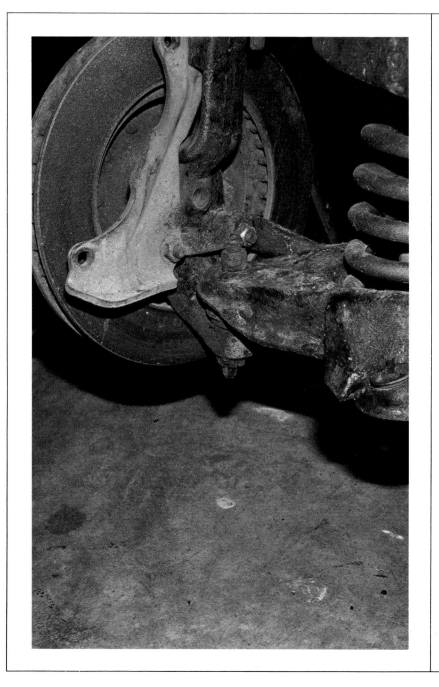

Left: Even a chassis in this condition reveals much to the alert restorer. Differences in the type of retainers are evident, as are the variances in gloss and texture of black chassis components. A painted inspection code is still visible on the lower end of the spindle.
Above: Dave Burroughs prefers a mild cleaning technique to avoid destroying a Corvette's identity. Here he uses a soft brass brush and soapy water to expose the serial number stamped into the frame rail.

Above: A correct state-of-the-art restoration strives to preserve date codes, serial numbers, inspection marks, and other things which create a unique identity for each Corvette built. Here a stenciled part number, covered with years of road dirt accumulation, is barely visible.
Below: After careful cleaning with a soft brush and soapy water, the number emerges, as well as another below it. The part numbers were applied by the frame's manufacturer, the A.O. Smith Company.

Above: Closer view of the stenciled numbers shows that when they were applied, the stencil slipped, creating a double image. Before removing the numbers, Dave Burroughs matched the stencil lettering style and made his own stencil for later duplication, including the slip!
Below: Overall view shows the location of the stenciled part numbers. They are on the passenger side frame rail, and they were put in when the frame was inverted, so that they appear upside-down now.

this guide to reproduce the numbers by holding the plastic guide over the correct location, then peeling it back while still holding it in position by one edge. He'd make a number or part of one, then flip the guide back to check his work. Little by little, he recreated the original . . . not just the number, but in the right style, angle and location.

The same plastic template technique was used to duplicate hash marks Dave uncovered on the frame at each body mount location. These marks, made with a "lumber-crayon" paint pencil, were put on the frame before the body was lowered on. They indicated how many shims were required.

What happened at the factory was that the operator who determined how many shims were required marked the frame. For Dave's frame, a white mark meant one shim. An orange mark at the core support mount meant five shims. So rather than mark eight slash marks for eight shims, the operator marked one orange and three white. The person who actually installed the shims temporarily taped them into position so they wouldn't fall off before the body was set on. The shim-holding tape on Dave's car looked like wide black masking tape. It was still in place, but it couldn't be reused because the stickum was shot. Dave was able to find a whole roll of tape that matched perfectly. He reapplied it just as the factory had done.

Missing factory hash marks for shim placement and missing black or tan masking tape are two additional "gotchas" that might reveal a clever restoration that is being passed off as an untouched original. In the past, the common fraud in the Corvette world was the "original fuel injected" Corvette that wasn't. Trends come and go, and the trend of the future appears to be the original low mileage Corvette. Scarcity influences value, and they are scarce. Extending this logic, the valuable restoration will be the one that duplicates the original as closely as possible. Maybe, maybe not. The arguments favoring this happening are certainly strong.

Does the lack of shim marks on the frame, or the lack of tape holding them in place mean the car is not authentic? Not at all. Just understand the possibilities. If you were inspecting a Corvette claimed to be original in every respect, but could find no shim marks or tape on a relatively clean chassis, what would this mean? Does it mean that this is one of those very rare Corvettes that didn't require any shims? No. Even if shims weren't required, the chassis was marked with a "O." But it might mean that the body was pulled by an amateur who didn't know what the shims were and didn't bother to replace them. Disaster.

There are additional possibilities. If you can see shims in place, but no tape or marks, maybe a previous owner just removed the tape and marks because he didn't like the looks of them. This is fairly common in concours-prepared Corvettes. It could also mean the body has been removed. Very few Corvette restorers up to now have bothered to wrap tape around the shims before putting the body back on. You'll know if you pull the body yourself. There's no way to remove the tape from the surface between the top of the shim and the body mounts without lifting the body.

What all this means is this. You can't make any rock-bottom conclusions when a car you're looking at has or doesn't have shim marks, or some tape still in place at the shim locations. These are just two more bits of information to program into your mental computer. If you understand how all these bits of information fit together, you'll be much more able to evaluate a Corvette under consideration for purchase. If you're already restoring your Corvette, the information will help you understand what you're seeing as your car comes apart, and will assist you in putting it back together again. More than anything, understanding things like shim placement underscores the importance of documentation. If your Corvette is just as it should be, and you restore it correctly, document what you started with and what you did. If you don't document and you want to sell your car some day in the future, you'll have to convince a skeptical buyer verbally. Overwhelm him with a few hundred photos instead.

One of the more interesting conclusions Dave reached with regard to chassis restoration was that a number of different black paints and coatings must be used on various chassis parts to duplicate the natural factory look. This is because several types of coatings were used and application methods by numerous suppliers varied. For instance, some parts were sprayed while others were dipped. Some were baked, some were not. Dave realized that just looking into the engine compartment alone, you should see six to eight different gloss gradations and color tones of black.

This sort of scrutiny indicates what sort of restoration Dave Burroughs was striving for. In the recent past, it was considered pretty good if a restorer managed to get the right parts painted the right color. Burroughs took it to the extreme of using the correct type of paint or coating and then applying it correctly to duplicate slight differences in color and even texture and solubility. More details on this later in the discussion of restoration.

Most restorers know that GM stamped the Corvette's serial number into the frame at several locations. GM is actually quite secretive about this practice and you're not likely to find much written about it, especially in anything where GM is the source. The reason is that the numbers are there for theft identification. Thieves are proficient at switching ID plates, or even making their own. But they usually don't have the time to bother changing numbers stamped in the chassis. Even if they did, changing numbers stamped into steel is no easy task. When police or insurance representatives need positive identification of a vehicle, they can refer to confidential material that directs them to "secret" locations on the frame where the serial number is stamped.

Mis-stamped frames, serial tags, and engines have all been documented by restorers.

GM didn't put the numbers in the frame for the restorers' benefit, but it's nice they are there. Matching numbers removes practically all doubt that a body and chassis left the factory together.

If the numbers don't match, it just about has to be for one of three reasons. First, the car was involved in a theft and the serial tags on the body were switched. Which means that the body and chassis might well be the original combination. Second, the frame has been switched due to a rust-out or collision. There might not be anything wrong with those possibilities, but it's sure nice to know. The third possibility is that GM made an error. It does happen. GM may be the largest auto firm in the United States, but that doesn't mean it isn't capable of mistakes. Because of the seriousness of the matter, GM is very careful and certainly errors are rare. But mis-stamped frames, serial tags, and engines have all been documented by restorers.

Dave Burroughs uncovered his frame's serial numbers with a soft brass brush. The numbers can be obscured by frame coating, dirt, and rust buildup, but if you know where to look they can almost always be exposed. Dave photographed the numbers as part of his ongoing documentation.

As Dave progressed through disassembly he kept a chart with the location, size, head markings, type (code), length and other data for every bolt, nut, and retainer removed. Corvette chassis bolts and nuts are normally either raw steel, cadmium plated, or zinc plated, and Dave made note of that as well. How do you tell which is which? Raw steel is pretty obvious. You'll get to know cadmium and zinc after a while, but the definitive test is to submerge a questionable item in muriatic acid. If it's zinc, it will bubble. If it's cadmium, no bubbles.

Dave grouped like retainers in trays and cleaned and refinished them as necessary. His chart system assured that every retainer (we're including nuts and bolts and any other fasteners in this heading) would wind up back in the correct location. That is to say that the correct type of retainer would get back in the right location, not necessarily the exact same one.

Putting each and every retainer exactly back where it came from is difficult but not impossible. The merits of doing this are debatable, but it could be done with an extensive tray and tag system. The danger here is that your plater could scramble the trays and tags and you're lost. Dave's system of just identifying what type of retainer used at each location eliminated this possibility.

Dave did conceive another idea for getting each retainer back where it came from. What you do is have a series of metal plates which are drilled and tapped appropriately. You screw each bolt into a properly identified location . . . What's neat about this idea is that you can give the entire assembly . . . plate with bolts screwed in . . . to your plater. He plates everything so nothing can get lost. There are a couple of problems though. The portion of the threads actually touching the plate won't be plated.

As you can see, there's practically no end to the extent you can take a restoration. And no matter how high you set your goals, there is a way to achieve them.

Some restorers believe in replacing "every nut and bolt."

Above: Corvette chassis components contain numerous codes, markings, and other assembly clues evident only to those willing to look for them. Note the remains of a green part number tag on the front coil spring, and to the right of this tag, mysterious dribbles of a hardened goo found in similar locations on many mid-year Sting Rays.
Below: Easy to miss, but yellow inspection marks are still visible on the steering knuckle.

Above: This is the crossmember which ''carries'' the differential. Though it appeared rusty, soap and water cleanup brought it to this state. Part numbers have been exposed, and also the triangular stamped logos of the manufacturer, barely visible above the numbers.
Below: The green stripe on the driveshaft clearly shows through the dirt. Factory assembly manuals specify that the paint mark on the driveshaft is to be aligned with the paint mark on the pinion flange.

By carefully cleaning down to the red primer under the fenderwells, Dave Burroughs was able to determine how much of this underbody area was painted. In fact, by studying differences in the paint patterns between the passenger and driver sides, Dave was able to conclude that they were sprayed by a right-handed employee spraying in a counterclockwise motion.

Should you? There is no reason to. You'll round a few bolt heads, strip a thread or two, and maybe snap some bolts off. But if you can salvage a part and it is perfectly serviceable, why not use it again?

The same philosophy holds true for many chassis components, but some do wear out. Anywhere there is a grease fitting, parts are moving against something and wear is possible. The springs in your Corvette are also parts that may well deserve replacement. They can wear out from just the car's weight on them over a period of years and top spring performance is critical to a Corvette's handling performance.

In the simplest terms, chassis disassembly is a matter of unbolting things and keeping track of where they came from. There are things along the way that can be done incorrectly and can cause confusion and difficulty in the assembly stage. These are head-scratchers that are frustrating, but they're seldom dangerous. It goes without saying that care and common sense have to be exer-

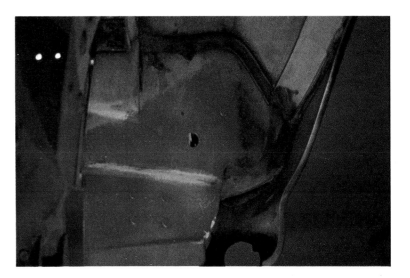

cised during the body lift and engine pull. Getting under the chassis always requires proper blocking, but even the most amateur restorer is aware of that. The one item of chassis disassembly that can fool some people is spring removal. It can be downright dangerous.

1963 and later Corvettes have coil springs in front and a single, transverse leaf at the rear. All earlier Corvettes have the coils at the front and two leaf springs at the rear in conventional fashion. Chevrolet introduced a plastic rear leaf in the 1981 model Corvette (automatic transmission), but it functioned the same as earlier steel units and requires the same precautions.

If you've never removed a spring before, have someone with you who has. If you can't get the proper tools, let someone else do the job for you. Springs are under tremendous pressure. If you don't know what you're doing and simply start unbolting things, an unrestrained spring could let loose and injure you seriously. The job is done correctly by restraining the spring with a special tool. In a Corvette, the front coil springs are positioned between the upper and lower control arms. With the tool restraining the spring, the lower control arm can be disconnected by unbolting the spindle from the upper control arm ball joint stud. Before removing the nut completely from the stud, striking the spindle will release the spindle from the stud, but the nut will still restrain the control arm. By increasing tension on the spring compressor, the tension on the control arm is released and the nut can be safely removed. The danger is that someone not familiar with the procedure might be tempted to carefully unscrew the nut and see what happens. Because of the tight tapered fit, the assembly might not let loose until tapped a few times. But when it does let loose, it could do so with enough force to take an arm off. Rear leafs are less lethal because of the limited distance one end can go when released, but they still deserve the same respect.

Every restorer who's been through this a few times develops techniques for spring removal and often fashions his own tools. A floor jack properly positioned will do nicely on a rear leaf, for instance. If the body is off the chassis, the whole spring removal business gets much simpler and safer because of the excellent access. Because of the dangers involved, this is one area that you are advised to refer to the GM service manual and to go by the "book" if it's your first time through. Understand that it can be done differently, with different tools and with complete safety. Just don't try it yourself initially.

With all due cautions explained, the question of replacement arises. Should new springs be installed, or should the old ones be used again. No one should criticise a Corvette restoration that has had springs replaced as being non-original. Springs wear out like tires wear out. You certainly want the correct replacement springs, and getting rid of the worn-out ones is no less proper than replacing rotted tires with NOS rubber.

Any Corvette more than a decade old is a candidate for spring replacement. The exception is the genuine low mileage original, especially one that's been stored "on blocks." The whole idea of putting a car up this way for extended periods of time is to support the weight by the frame, not the suspension. A mistake many restorers make is to assume that since their Corvette was level, the springs must be all right. That's archaic thinking. If a car is leaning, surely it does have a suspension problem. But springs can be very tired and still keep a car level, especially the rear single leaf of Corvette Sting Rays.

Spring replacement is another one of those personal judgement calls. Even though the Burroughs-Ellefsen '65 had over 80,000

miles on it, Dave used the originals because the car's ground clearance was still within factory tolerances. Some restorers automatically replace springs, shocks, ball joints, and any other suspension components that even hint of being suspicious.

Regardless of your decision, remember this: Never replace one coil spring without replacing the other side. If it was leaning to the left, it will wind up leaning to the right. The same thing holds true for the leaf springs of 1962 and older Corvettes.

You can replace front springs without replacing rears, but be prepared for trouble because you could wind up with just the opposite of the condition you're trying to correct. Replacing the fronts because the car sags often results in a car sagging in the rear.

There are little devices made to lower and raise springs. These take the form of little clamps to squeeze the coils and, more often, blocks to spread them. Avoid these things. They are temporary fixes and have no place on a Corvette, certainly not on a Corvette restoration. If your budget requires some economizing, you can consider having a spring shop rebuild your leaf springs by replacing damaged or weak leaves. This is a dying art, so be confident of the people you're dealing with.

Engine Disassembly

Pulling an engine is terribly frightening the first time. Those who have done it have all been through it. "If I take this electrical line off, will it short out? Will it blow up?" It all seems funny later, but very intimidating at the time. Disconnect the battery and nothing will short out. Follow the sequence outlined in the Chevrolet service manual and things will go smoothly. Above all, take your time and don't rush it.

As was earlier indicated, Dave Burroughs prefers to pull the engine from the chassis before the body is off. Dave has removed engines from Corvettes so many times he has it down to a science. When he started, Dave would follow the service manual closely. Here's what the manual says you should do:
1. Drain cooling system and crankcase.
2. Scribe line around hood hinges and remove hood.

3. Remove air cleaner and cover carburetor with cloth.
4. Remove distributor shielding.
5. Remove shroud and radiator as outlined.
6. Disconnect:
   a. Battery cables at battery.
   b. Wires at starter solenoid.
   c. Delcotron wiring.
   d. Engine-to-body ground straps.
   e. Oil pressure indicator at engine.
   f. Temperature indicator lead at sending switch.
   g. Coil primary lead at coil.
   h. Tachometer cable at distributor.
   i. Gas tank line at fuel pump.
   j. Accelerator rod at pedal bellcrank and TV rod (lower) at TV bellcrank.
   k. Heater hose at engine connections, and remove from clip at generator bracket.
   l. Power brake hose at carburetor "T."
7. Remove fan and fan pulley assemblies.
8. Power steering only:
   a. Remove power steering pump mount bolts and swing pump into radiator opening or:
   b. Disconnect pump lines and plug open ends.

9. Remove rocker arm covers.
10. Remove distributor cap, move it forward of distributor and and cover distributor with a cloth.
11. Raise vehicle and place on jack stands.
12. Disconnect exhaust pipes at manifold flanges.
13. Remove oil filter.
14. Block clutch pedal in up position, then remove clutch cross-shaft (frame bracket end first, then slide off engine ball stud).
15. Remove starter assembly.
16. Remove flywheel cover plate (Synchromesh) or converter underpan (Powerglide).
17. Remove engine front mount through bolts.
18. Position a floor jack under transmission, then remove all but top 2 bell housing-to-engine bolts.
19. Install engine lift tool, then remove two upper bell housing bolts.
20. Powerglide Only- Remove flywheel-to-converter bolts and install converter holding bracket to transmission.
21. Raise and move engine forward alternately as needed to remove engine from vehicle.
22. Install engine on engine stand and remove lift tool assembly.

There's nothing wrong with the GM procedure for a novice restorer. It provides a thorough check list and step-by-step directions. For someone who has done this a zillion times like Dave Burroughs, there is a better way. The GM procedure (this is from the '63 service manual) takes you under the car several times. All the things listed have to be done, but Dave puts the car on jackstands first, then crawls under just once with all the tools he'll need to do everything required underneath. When he emerges, the jackstands come out and he does everything under the hood. The time savings realized by not having to go back under the car several times are significant.

Normally, deviating from GM suggested procedure isn't worth the effort. In Dave's case it was because he had the 396 engine in and out of a test car five times for testing, inspecting, and re-restoration purposes.

Stage Three: Research and Restoration

Research and restoration are different elements of a Corvette restoration, yet research occurs simultaneously with disassembly and especially with the actual restoration of components. The best example of Dave's approach to combining research into his project was his fascination with coatings.

Dave Burroughs was not content to determine what color parts were painted, or what type of plating was used. He wanted to know what coatings were used and how they were applied.

He doesn't take a preachy attitude about this. His own '67 silver coupe, the car that won its class at Bloomington, McDorman's and the NCCC convention at Orlando in 1976, is not restored according to the techniques he now advocates. Every chassis part that was black was finished in a uniform satin black monotone. The car was and still is gorgeous. But the only thing that really differentiated it from other well restored Corvettes was the degree of perfection. It competed with other Corvettes on the basis of craftsmanship, not authenticity, and this began to bother Dave Burroughs and others who think like him.

It wasn't an instant decision or revelation. But over time and after many discussions, he was ultimately convinced that a natural factory look was the correct restoration goal to pursue. When Dave started his project, one that was to take three years, it was with a sense of mission. The few remaining genuine low mileage originals were rare and becoming rarer. The time had come.

The change in restoration goals also dictates a change in the type of book describing start-of-the-art restoration. Five years ago, any restoration book worth its salt would have devoted half the text to body refinish techniques. Many people look no further than a snazzy paint job in evaluating a restoration. Now those who know look much deeper.

Certainly a Corvette's outward appearance is still very important. But the mystery of how to make it look flawless is no mystery anymore. You can take your Corvette to any qualified body shop and, provided you pay them enough, they'll give you a perfect paint job. They don't even need to know a single thing about Corvettes.

This is part of the reason for the dramatic shift in emphasis in the type of Corvette restoration done by Dave Burroughs and others who recognize that this is an art, not just a task. Making something that has aged look pretty is a task. Making it look just like it looked when it was originally built is restoration . . . and restoration is an art.

The most dramatic evidence of state-of-the-art restoration in the Burroughs-Ellefsen '65 is in the chassis. This is not because the chassis is restored "better" than the body, but because the difference in accuracy between their effort and most previous Corvette restorations is much more noticeable in the chassis area than in the body.

Body finish on the Burroughs-Ellefsen Corvette would be viewed differently by different peer levels of onlookers. The car looks just like it would have looked in 1965 resting comfortably in a Chevy dealer's showroom. So to the average man on the street, it looks like new. There is another level of people who know automobiles and quality. Just as this type of person would have found flaws in the showroom example in 1965, he'll find them in the Burroughs-Ellefsen restoration as well. He'll note that panel fits are not perfect. Overspray will be present. Some fiberglass panels will not be perfectly smooth. There may be a hint of a fiberglass joining seam. Orange peel will be evident in some sections of the exterior paint.

There is one more level of expertise. This is the person who knows Corvettes so well that he realizes that every flaw in the Burroughs-Ellefsen restoration is typical of factory production. This isn't shoddy work, this is accuracy. If you know what you're looking at, it'll take your breath away.

The photos accompanying this text tell the story best, but some specifics relating to the body are in order.

Body

After studying the body of his '65 Corvette project carefully at the outset, Dave concluded that not every square inch of it had to be refinished. There were areas that were in excellent condition and warranted preservation for historical reasons.

One was the underside of the hood. In the past, restored Corvettes have had this area finished to perfection. This gives the car a phony cosmetic look that no assembly plant would bother with. Dave also wanted to preserve some of the historical identity of such things as raw fiberglass under the hood hinges which indicates that the underhood area was painted with the hinges in place. It could be refinished the same way, but what's the purpose?

This early '65 396 convertible also had displayed what surely was a do-it-yourself trim job across the top of the radiator support for hood clearance. It actually looked like it was done with a hacksaw and not done very well because some rough edges contacted the inner hood and forced it up on the right side. The rough trim left little "teeth" marks where it was holding the hood up.

Prior to the emphasis on natural factory look, a Corvette restorer would have taken one peek at the ragged trim on the radiator support and shook his head in disgust. He would have pulled the radiator support and ground down the top edge for clearance. Then he'd have repaired the gouge marks and refinished the inner hood. Then he would have aligned the hood perfectly.

Early 396 Corvette engine installations required a hand trim operation of the radiator support because of interference with the inner hood. It didn't look great, but that's how the factory had to do it until a fix could be engineered in. A restorer who removes

The areas under the attaching screws of this unrestored '65 rear filler panel are not painted, nor were the screws themselves painted. This apparent contradiction happened because the factory temporarily hung the panel on the car for painting, then removed it, put it in a rack, then later attached it to the car (or another of the same color) with new screws. Because of its location when painted, coverage varied from a heavy dripping upper coat, to thin coverage at the lower edges.

the evidence in the interest of cosmetic attractiveness is destroying a part of the character and identity of his Corvette. Harsh words perhaps, but obvious to anyone who truly understands the magic of the Corvette mystique. This is the kind of error made by the restorer who plunges in, the restorer who ignores the initial documentation and scrutiny phase.

Another panel that Dave chose not to refinish was the rear filler panel, that piece that is across the rear of mid-year Corvettes below the bumpers. The filler panel has the recess area for the license plate and the round holes for exhaust exit (except for side-exhaust optioned models).

There have been aspects of this particular body panel that have stumped Corvette restorers for years, at least those restorers who've taken the time to study the panel's paint patterns. What is baffling is that on an original car it can be noted that the screws holding the panel on are not painted. This would seem to indicate that the filler panel is not painted while attached to the car. Yet when the pristine holding screws are removed, the areas under the screws are raw fiberglass . . . screws had to be in place when the panel was painted. Overspray on the inner lip of the rear fenders where they mate to the filler panels also confirm that something was in place when the fenders were painted, because part of the lip will not have overspray. If nothing was in place, the entire lip would be covered with paint. But why just part of it?

Given these facts, most restorers in the past have concluded that the filler panel was in place when the car was painted and that somewhere along the line the screws have been replaced or cleaned. It seems ridiculous to believe that the factory would have done it.

But they did. Remember that when the Corvette body was painted at St. Louis, it had not yet been mated to the chassis. When the two do meet, the rear filler panel cannot be on the car, because it would interfere with the frame at the time of body drop. What the factory did was to temporarily hang the filler panel in position. It was not fully seated and thus the inner lip of the rear fender mating area was partially shielded from overspray. After the body was painted, the panel was removed and the screws pitched. When it finally went back on after the body drop, new screws were used to attach it.

The rear filler panel mystery is just one of many examples of something in which Dave Burroughs invested hours of research and phone time. And Dave credits Mike Hanson of Chicago with figuring this one out. Once he understood how it was done, it was not difficult for Dave to duplicate the spray patterns on the filler panel. But it was in excellent shape, so he decided to just leave it alone in the interest of authenticity.

The decision to leave the panel alone caused a problem which illustrates a caution that has been mentioned before. Dave forgot to mask off the portions of the taillight panel that would have been covered by the filler panel's temporary location for painting. The caution is that when you send your body to the paint shop, everything exposed will be painted. You can't expect your painters to spot your masking errors and correct them. If they're good, they'll assume that you've set the car up exactly the way you want it in terms of overspray.

Interior

For the most part, Corvette enthusiasts profit by the high level of interest in the hobby of preserving and restoring Corvettes. Several companies have entered the business of supplying this market, making available many parts that were simply not obtainable a few years ago. But no business blossoms with only sweet flowers, and the Corvette world has had more than its fair share of crooks, cheats, and worse. There have been many cases of severe disappointment in merchandise, and more than a few instances of prepaid merchandise never arriving.

Time has a way of sorting this out and the present level of parts availability and quality has never been better. Granted, companies still exist which specialize in junk merchandise and horrible customer relations. But they're the minority and as the word gets around, maybe they'll go away, too.

The biggest problem area for the restorer of a Corvette a few years ago was the total unavailability of interior soft-ware parts. Corvette seats have never been the greatest for durability. The molded-in armrests that started with the '65 models were nice to look at but cracked if you used them more than a few times.

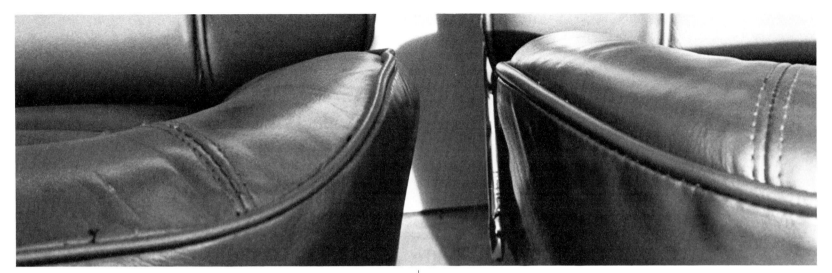

Carpeting wears out in any car, but the Corvette's tendency to be less than waterproof, especially in convertible form, exaggerated even that problem. In short, if you owned a Corvette and wanted to restore it or just spruce it up, your interior options were very limited.

This created an incredible dilemma for Corvette restorers. Of all the parts in the GM inventory, interior parts are the first to be dropped from service warehouses. They're bulky, they don't store well, and they're not necessary for the operation of the vehicle. Enthusiasts found local interior trim shops incapable of matching materials and stitching. About the only hope was the swap meet and that's precisely the reason why Bloomington and other meets met with such success. This was a parts-hungry market.

Starting around 1974, things started changing. New cars were feeling the worst of the emission mandates and engineers were up to their necks just building cars legal to sell. Enthusiasts did the obvious and turned back the calendar to the great cars of the fifties and sixties. Few were better than Corvettes, and the interest renewal sparked several phenomenons.

Prices soared. There was a period of time when Corvette value increases exceeded any other investment imaginable . . . di-amonds, gold, housing, whatever. A score of publications sprung up to satisfy the thirst. Most importantly, businesses sprung up to sell the booming market anything it wanted. GM even got into the act, digging up old stamping dies and cranking out obsolete parts in high enthusiast demand.

One of the better outgrowths of all this was the increased availability of high quality interior parts. In fact, some of the interior parts are actually of higher quality than the parts they replace. That can be both good and bad as Dave Burroughs found out.

The Burroughs-Ellefsen '65 convertible came with a Bright Blue leather interior, coded #415. For a car that had in the neighborhood of 80,000 miles, the condition of the interior components was quite good. The carpeting was soiled but not excessively worn. Some seat seams were letting go, but there were no tears or worn areas in the leather. Best of all, the previous owners obviously hadn't used the armrests because the door panels were like new.

There's the dilemma. The original interior was quite nice, but the goal of the restoration was to bring the car back to the condition it was in when it left St. Louis. Nice as the interior was, it didn't have the natural factory look of a just-built car.

Dave decided on a compromise. Since the door panels were all right, they would be used. The carpet would be replaced, but the original underpad would be retained. The seats would be put away and kept for historical reference. A spare set of '65 seats were purchased and these were recovered in new leather.

The original intent of this plan was to keep the original interior parts not used in the restoration available for historical reference. The lesson to be applied to all restorations is that interior parts should always be saved regardless of condition. Dave was able to compare the reproductions to the originals and detect variances. Some he was able to work out with the manufacturer and some he was not.

Dave worked with a major Corvette interior supplier. He found their cooperation ran hot and cold. He wanted to buy interior parts that were very close matches to those which were being replaced.

The manufacturer maintained it didn't make sense to reproduce a part just like GM made it if GM made it wrong. For example, if a door panel had a design weakness that caused it to split, the manufacturer felt justified in changing the design. Realizing that most restorers put new seat covers over pads that had lost some shape, replacement covers were cut to fit squashed-out cushions, not originals. For example, in the case of Dave's '65 leather seats, this results in a rather flat reproduction seat, contrasted to the ''bat wing'' effect of the original.

There's no perfect answer to this. The manufacturers' position is understandable, but having his originals to compare to, Dave also found simple cases of reproduction error. He realizes that exact material duplicates may not be available and that colors may vary. He also realizes that manufacturing techniques and equipment limitations could dictate some variances. But he's hopeful that he can work with manufacturers to at least hold

dimensions as close as possible. He's generally satisfied with the quality level of interior components available, but feels there's still room for accuracy improvements.

An area that no interior manufacturer can be faulted is in color variance. Some colors are worse than others. Black is the safest, but even it can vary if the textures are different. Blue is a trouble color because of its inherent tendency to be a little too light or dark, or off-shade. Reproduction reds tend to be too bright, but fairly close in color. Saddles never seem to be right on.

In defense of suppliers, color matches are almost impossible and perhaps a matter of luck on your part if you can find them. The dye mixes vary now from batch to batch. And they varied when the cars were built. Compare two '65 models with original Bright Blue interiors and you may find they're not the same. True, they may not have aged simultaneously due to a difference in exposure to the elements. But you can always find some vinyl or leather that was hidden from exposure. Comparing even these areas will likely show some variance. The real topper is that you'll even find variance in the same car. Hard to explain, but it is true.

This presentation should start to give you a feel for what the manufacturer of Corvette restoration interior parts is up against and, more importantly, what a restorer seeking the natural factory look in his restoration is up against. If all this makes you want to start looking for an original Corvette with a perfect factory interior, you now understand why the purists are willing to pay such exorbitant prices for them. Maybe they're not so exorbitant after all.

Based on his experiences and frustrations with interior components, Dave offers these words of wisdom, caution, and advice. All of the following applies to the Burroughs-Ellefsen '65 model. Some of the information would be exclusive to the '65 while much would apply to other Corvettes.

If at all possible, deal with your interior parts supplier on a personal basis. Gather up the originals you want to replace and take them with you on a personal visit. Show the supplier what you need. The supplier may have several color gradations of materials in stock for you to choose from and match-up to your original. You have to sort of walk a tightrope in that you don't want to come off as a pain in the neck. You want to appear to be a

The portion of the seat belt near the buckle latch is typically subjected to the most wear, but the portion hidden inside the retractor cover will be like new. Though it requires removing the manufacturer's tag and considerable restitching, the belt can be switched end for end.

genuine enthusiast interested in restoring your car with correct materials. You should be willing to pay a little extra for the supplier's extra effort. One thing to always remember is that most people in the Corvette replacement parts business are or were Corvette enthusiasts themselves. Strike up the proper relationship and most will bend over backwards to help you.

If the seat belts require replacement in your restoration, you may have difficulty locating something suitable. Dave devised a neat little trick for salvaging the worn belts in his '65. The belt setup consisted of a console retainer for the inner belts which have the buckles attached, and a roll-up mechanism for the outer belts. The outer belt on the driver side showed the most wear but Dave discovered that there was about six inches of belt hidden in the plastic retractor cover that has never seen the light of day . . . it was perfect. What Dave did is turn the belt end for end. This requires some disassembly, including unstitching the metal tongue that slips into the buckle and the IRVING AIR CHUTE identification tag. But the result is that you wind up with a cosme-

tically perfect belt that also happens to be the one that came with the car. Unfortunately, the same trick probably won't work on the inner belts which have the buckles attached. Switching these will bring some fresh belts to the buckle end, but it will be hidden by the top layer of belt as it passes through the buckle.

You might get lucky and find NOS seat belts and other interior parts at a Corvette swap meet. Though GM didn't keep interior parts available for long, they had to be available for a while and some have been tucked away. The rarest of interior parts do surface occasionally.

The seat belt buckle can be refinished if necessary by a cosmetic paint freshen-up. Dave did repaint his and also replaced the little circular bow tie emblem with a reproduction currently available. Be aware that this reproduction bow tie emblem has a slightly different satin background, but is otherwise excellent.

Pedals are another example of interior parts that wear out and have to be dealt with in a restoration. Original Corvette pedals tend to wear well, but if a previous owner liked to "heel and toe" between the brake and accelerator, the edge of the brake pedal can be badly worn. There are loads of reproduction pedals floating around which look fine though they're not coded properly on the inside surface. GM has replacement pedals available and they'll fit properly but the design most likely won't match your originals. Buy what you can get, save your originals, and keep your eyes peeled for NOS pedals.

Interior parts that have painted surfaces, such as the seat belt buckles, the heater ducts and the fiberglass panels that cover the folding top mechanisms of convertibles, can be successfully refinished with paint that can still be purchased at local jobbers. Dave went to his local Dupont auto paint store, found the correct color listed in the interior paint catalog, and the paint was custom mixed on the spot. It was an excellent match.

One last tidbit relating to interiors. On mid-year Corvettes, you'll often find an unusual striped pattern on the footwells of both the driver and passenger sides after the carpet and pad have been pulled out. The color of the stripes will match the car's exterior paint. Know what it is? It's where the factory sprayed the little air intake grills that are just forward of the windshield. That's right. The grills were not sprayed in position on the car

because the pockets under them wouldn't get any paint. A handy place to put them was on the bare fiberglass floors. As the painter opened the doors to get to the jambs, he just leaned in and gave the vents a shot. That's why the hold-down phillips-head screws are not painted but the area under them is. That's a little piece of factory folklore that has had more than one restorer scratching his head. Now you know. To verify on your own mid-year, just remove the vent and place it on the corresponding floor. The spray pattern will line up perfectly.

Chassis

After disassembly had been completed, Dave studied components and confirmed suspicions he already had. To be correct, chassis components (and others) had to be refinished with different materials and different techniques. Nowhere was this more evident than with black parts such as brackets and chassis items. Dave's procedure was straightforward. Before and after removing a part, he'd carefully note its appearance. If there were streaks in the part, which direction did they go? If there was puddling, at which end was it concentrated? What was the degree of gloss on the part and what sort of texture did it have? How durable was the coating and what solvents would dissolve it?

Sometimes researching the part that came off the car was not enough. In these cases, Dave went further. He tried to buy a new-old-stock duplicate to clear the mystery. Having made Corvette friends across the country, he knew where low mileage originals of the same vintage as his were located. He made trips as necessary to observe them, again taking voluminous notes and photographs.

Dave was concerned with virtually every chassis component, but using a front bumper bracket as an example, Dave observed that there were lines on one end of the part. The lines indicated that a heavy coat of paint was applied and the puddling showed in what position the part hung as the paint ran, collected at the end, then dried. Dave cannot say conclusively that such a part was dipped or heavily sprayed. What he could say was that he couldn't reproduce the look by spraying, but he could by dipping.

Left: As much as any photo, this one captures the essence of the Burroughs-Ellefsen restoration. The bumper bracket to the left is restored, the other is an original NOS part. The paint streaks, created when the paint ran while drying, are faithfully recreated. So is the collection of paint along the right edge, culminating in a hardened drip at the corner. Observe also the duplication of not only the correct black gloss, but its texture as well.
Above: This is another view of the same brackets shown at left. The surface integrity is correct, but the light scratches were not reproduced because they are not indicative of the part as installed.

(By the way, the bumper bracket is one of the parts that Dave purchased an extra in NOS form to verify his observations.)

Dave found that the finish of the bumper brackets could be duplicated with a readily available product from GM. It's called GM Reconditioning paint, part number 1050104. Thanks due again here to Mike Hanson, the expert restorer in the Chicago area, who supplied the information to Dave. Mike shares Dave's fascination with chassis finishes and has been delving into finish mysteries for quite some time. Coincidentally, this is the same Mike Hanson who brought the '65 feature restoration back to Chicago and sold it to Don Ellefsen and Dave Burroughs.

It was the attention to detail that makes the Burroughs-Ellefsen restoration so special. Things like the little aluminum band wrap-

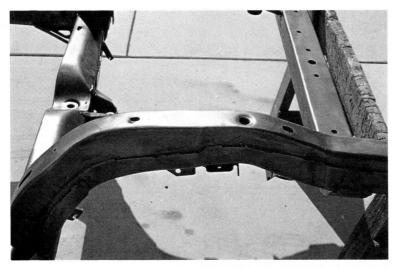

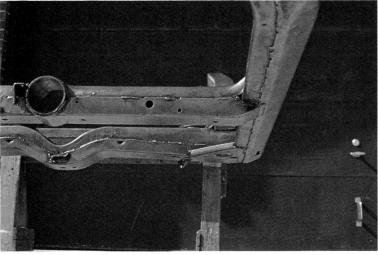

These are documentation photos illustrating the authenticity and integrity of the Burroughs-Ellefsen '65 frame before refinishing. The serial number shown as left is barely visible in the top photo as well. The area shown is the kickup for the rear wheel. The number is also stamped into the frame at another location further forward on the side frame rail. In all shots, note the degree of weld splatter and cratering. For authenticity, these should not be cosmetically enhanced.

ped around the brake lines going to the master cylinder. It serves no apparent purpose. It often gets removed and thrown away, especially if a line is replaced. But some thinking and research reveal why it's there. The brake lines were in place on the chassis before the body was dropped on at the factory. The band was there to temporarily hold the lines until they could be hooked up to the master cylinder. Once the brake lines are hooked up, the band becomes useless. But it hurts nothing to be there so the factory leaves it.

Dave didn't have parts sandblasted, preferring to clean components with less devastating methods. The driveshaft was one of many chassis components including the frame itself that Dave used wire brushes spun by a benchgrinder or drill motor to remove paint and light corrosion. But first came soap and water.

On the rear of the driveshaft he noted a green stripe. He cleaned and wire brushed around the stripe, then freshened it up with green paint. The stripe is there for a reason and the reason is spelled out in the 1965 assembly manual, page E-144. It says: NOTE: WHEN ASSEMBLING PROP SHAFT TO DIFFERENTIAL CARRIER, POSITION THE PAINT MARK ON THE PROP SHAFT IN LINE WITH THE PAINT MARK ON THE PINION FLANGE. Sure enough, Dave found the corresponding

Left: This number was handwritten onto the frame at St. Louis assembly, apparently the date when the frame was pulled from inventory and started down the line. The date corresponds to a Friday and the car was completed on the following Monday, April 12th.
Above: This is the handwritten date number as restored by Dave Burroughs using the orange lumber pencil resting on top of the frame. Dave used a plastic template technique illustrated on the next page to duplicate the number and even the writing style of the person who originally put it in.

mark, a blue dot, on the pinion flange. Dave hasn't determined what the specific colors mean, but they do vary. A '67 L-88 he's observed has an orange slash over a green slash on the driveshaft.

Additional factory paint coding can be observed on the brake calipers. Dave's calipers all had white dots. On a 1979 visit to the factory, Dave noted that brake calipers were still getting color codes, probably some sort of picking sequence.

The factory used little green clips on the brake lines of Dave's '65 to keep them attached to the frame. Dave matched the paint color exactly with zinc chromate paint obtained at the local airport maintenance shack. It is very important to use a rust inhibiting paint on these parts because nothing touching a brake line should breed corrosion. It's a good idea to dip these little clips to assure good coverage, then bake them to assure durability.

Dave noticed other interesting things as he disassembled his chassis. On the back surface of the rear frame crossmember, there was a series of bumps. Dave thought they were spotwelds. But as he started carefully cleaning with solvent, bumps would disappear. It turns out they were actually hardened drips of frame coating. But why on the back edge and not on the bottom? Because the frame was painted in the upright position, obviously with the front end at the top. As the asphalt-base frame coating dried, the drips formed and hardened.

You can bet a restored frame won't have these bumps. They are very hard to duplicate. Dave removed just a few before he realized what they were. He experimented with a wet spray technique but wasn't satisfied with the results. Since the crossmember was in excellent condition, he decided to clean around the "bumpies" and repaint right over them to leave them intact. Looking back, he now thinks he could have duplicated them by dabbling them in individually with a thick consistency of chassis paint.

On the subject of frame paint, Dave also made some interesting discoveries. He noticed that some chassis coatings, such as the frame itself, dissolved with gasoline. Other parts wouldn't. Some would dissolve easily with lacquer thinner, others were practically immune to lacquer thinner and even paint strippers. This means at least two things. First, the coatings applied are not the same materials. Second, some of the coatings are probably baked on. That's about the only way they could survive both lacquer thinner and paint strippers, though some components in close proximity with the engine could get a baking of sorts under the hood.

Since the frame coating thinned with gasoline, it was obviously petroleum based. This type is used because it is easy to apply, is a decent rust inhibitor, and it's cheap. It is not particularly durable and if GM's intent had been to prevent frame rustout in northern climates, they could have done much better.

Not only was the frame coating not chosen for real rust protection, but its application was more cosmetic than rust preventative too. The Corvette frame is a box section which means the main frame members are hollow squarish tubes. The box isn't sealed and it shouldn't be. 1963 frames have more of a tendency to rust out than later frames because of the addition of drainage holes to later frames. But if GM had been seriously concerned about frame

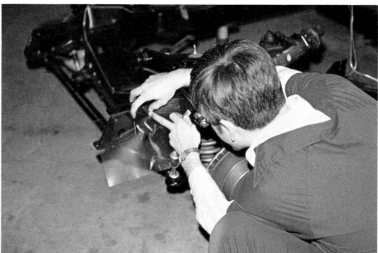

Above: *Dave Burroughs is shown starting to remark the frame for shim placement. At the forward mount, an orange slash meant five shims, a white mark one. Only white marks appeared at the other locations.*
Below: *Before removing old shim marks, Dave traced them onto a piece of clear plastic. Here, with the plastic properly located, he checks to see that each mark is correctly positioned, then lifts the plastic out of the way and proceeds to the next mark.*

Above: *Marking the shim placements continues. Be aware that there are some inconsistencies in factory coding. The combination of orange and white marks won't be seen on all Corvettes. Also, the number of shims actually found may not correspond exactly to what is marked, possibly due to an oversight on the part of the factory.*
Right: *The last mark goes on, skipping across a frame hole just as the original did.*

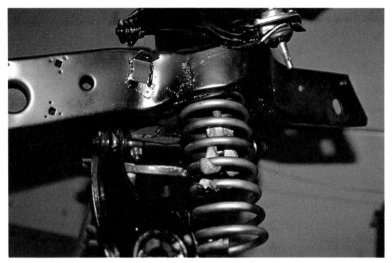

Above: This is the refinished A.O. Smith stenciled part number. Compare this to the original shown on page 37. Dave Burroughs even duplicated the "slip" of the original by allowing his template to slide while brushing the white paint over. The lettering is one inch Gothic.
Right: This is what state-of-the-art restoration is all about. Compare this photo with the unrestored view on page 36. There are three gradations of black. The chassis is one, the steering arm another, and the upper "A" arm still another. The weld cratering in the frame members has not been altered or camouflaged. Orange and white codes have been reproduced. Note also the excess sealant (shock base) which was allowed to drip and remain on the coil springs.

Above: In-process assembly photo of front suspension shows spring compressor in place. This tool squeezes the spring to allow assembly and disassembly.
Below: One feature of this photo is incorrect. The small oval flat on the spindle, just above and to the left of the retaining nut, is shown as being painted black. Because it was apparently machined after painting, the surface should be raw. It may even be rusty.

rust-out, all they had to do was specify that the frame manufacturer submerge the entire frame in a rust inhibitive liquid.

So why didn't they? The old cost bugaboo. In fairness to GM, it could be pointed out that a frame, rust or no rust, will almost always outlast a car's body and engine. So you can understand the GM beancounters' argument that money spent rustproofing a frame is money wasted.

True enough for most cars, but Corvettes are the exception. The Corvette body doesn't rust out and new life can be breathed into the engine perpetually. A worn out '65 Chevy four-door might fetch $50 at a junkyard, but try to buy any complete Corvette for less than a few thousand.

Left: *Both front and rear springs are under tremendous restraining force and the first time restorer is advised to seek assistance because spring removal and installation can be dangerous.*
Above: *Assembly continues. The white number on the differential has been freshened up along with the white bands on the rear trailing arms. The white bands on the trailing arms are not common and their significance is not certain. Dave Burroughs theorizes that they may have been rejected and marked, then corrected and installed later.*

Frame restoration and preservation should receive careful consideration in your restoration plan. If you're fortunate enough to have a southern or western car, and you expect to stay in the same area, restoration to GM's original specifications would certainly be in order. There may be no need to pull the body at all. If your frame is rusty and you plan to sandblast it, keep in mind that the blasting reaches only the outside surfaces. It also changes the look of the surface slightly and work hardens it in the process. The work hardening aspect won't affect much you do with chassis parts, but it can be an unpleasant surprise for the restorer of a metal body car who finds out later his dented fender resists straightening.

There's another way to get a rusted frame cleaned up. It's called chemical stripping and you may have seen advertisements for it by a company called Redi-Strip. There are others, but this one is well known because they cater to the auto restorer market.

Chemical stripping has been around in industrial circles for quite a while, but it's only recently that somebody has adapted the techniques to auto restorers and actively gone after the market. The exact formulas of the rust eaters used are closely guarded secrets of the companies doing the work, and the process is more than just a soaking in rust-eating acid. In fact, acid isn't even the correct term. Paint is stripped off in one tank, then a separate solution goes after the rust through an electrolytic action. The part gets washed down after each soak, and it goes back for more if any paint or rust remains. After it's cleaned up, it gets sprayed with a phosphate solution that etches the metal slightly and helps prevent surface rust from starting before you apply primer, paint or other coatings.

The beauty of chemical stripping for Corvette frames is that it gets to the inside surfaces where every other technique cannot. This is important because just like typical body rust, frame rust-through starts from the inside and works out.

But stripping isn't without its drawbacks. The process leaves residue which has to be cleaned up. Some of the gook used will creep out of seams and cracks for weeks. Sandblasters can be found in about any town in the country, but not necessarily so for

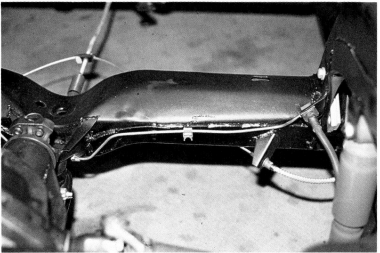

Above: This view of the differential shows the proper degree of restoration to chassis components, and the proper frame gloss. Visible to the left and right of the differential are the two eccentric cams at the inboard mountings of the strut rods. These are used to adjust the camber of the Corvette's independent rear suspension.
Below: This photo was taken from the differential looking forward. Note brake line retainer and yellow codes on the emergency brake cable.

Above: Restored transmission is simply cleaned with codes and markings freshened up or replaced. The car's serial number is stamped into the transmission vertically and is partially visible between the shifting rods. This is one of many ways to verify a Corvette's originality and specifically, that this transmission is the very one that was installed when the car was built.

the strippers. But with the general interest in restoration so strong, these dunk shops are proliferating and one may be closer than you think.

Another step you may wish to consider in preserving your frame, regardless of its original condition before you began, is rustproofing the interior surfaces. You can accomplish this by taking the frame to a commercial rustproofer such as Ziebart. A stripped down frame has enough access holes to permit a thorough rustproofing, providing the material used is one that creeps. Ziebart has always been acknowledged as one of the best, though surely there are others that are good. Just as surely, there are others that are lousy. Choose carefully. If you do decide to do this and your rustproofed chassis winds up on your garage floor, be sure to leave plenty of newspapers under it. Creeping rustproofers like Ziebart's seep and drip for weeks. It makes a mess, but your frame will last indefinitely.

This frame protection discussion would seem to contradict this book's position that natural factory look restorations are the state of the art, and that things must be done the way GM did them. But there are exceptions to everything and we make exception for two major categories. The frame is one and disc brakes, covered elsewhere in the text, the other. After all, the frame is critical to the longevity of the car, and both frame and brakes are critical safety items on cars to be driven. And there's nothing to stop you from putting a perfect factory match on the outside surfaces of the frame. The rustproofing with a Ziebart-type material should be on the inside only.

The Burroughs-Ellefsen '65 Corvette was a California car and hadn't been driven elsewhere other than a few summer months in Michigan when it was new. Chassis rust was practically nonexistent and neither Dave nor Don had any ideas of driving this car. Don may break down and give it a spin, but the chassis certainly will never see a drop of water. The goal was to create a zero mileage Corvette, not a driver. In keeping with these concepts, Dave decided to do the frame exactly as GM had. He located the original manufacturer of the frame coating and purchased a bulk quantity. For the individual restorer, this can be a problem because you can't go to the local hardware or auto shop and buy a quart of the stuff. Dave had to buy a drum, but he does plan to market it in smaller quantities to those who insist on having the correct material to refinish their frame or just do some authentic touch-up.

What you put on the outside surfaces on your frame is another of those argument-starting topics. Duplicating an original coating which is marginal at best in quality seems odd, especially so because far superior finishes are now available. It again comes down to what you're trying to achieve. If you want absolute factory originality, stay with it. If you're willing to deviate slightly in the direction of frame protection, you could compromise and use a superior frame coating followed by the original GM material. Your chassis will at least **look** correct.

Whatever you do, don't use something like Dupont's Imron® in gloss form and just leave it that way. Imron is a spectacular catalytic action paint with great durability. But it looks and feels wrong on a Corvette chassis. At the very least, put a dab of

dulling agent in it to kill the high gloss before applying. Better yet, follow it with an application of real chassis black.

During the course of his restoration, Dave visited the St. Louis Corvette assembly factory several times for in-depth study and note-taking. Many things have changed since the '65 models rolled down the line, but many things haven't. And there was always the possibility of talking to someone who was there in 1965 and remembers how the original Sting Rays were built. This brings up an important caution.

Throughout the restoration of the Burroughs-Ellefsen '65 Corvette, many very specific items were uncovered and many of these are included in this text. The caution is that what is correct for the feature car may not be correct for other Corvettes, or even other '65 Corvettes. In some ways, it is amazing how little Corvette production has changed over the years, but the reverse can also be said.

General Motors didn't build Corvettes with the convenience of a future restorer in mind.

Many things cause this. General Motors didn't build Corvettes with the convenience of a future restorer in mind. Can you imagine the plant manager of the Corvette factory shutting down the production line because a part wasn't available but a suitable replacement was? Someone pointing out that a substitution would confuse restorers a decade or two later would get laughed out of the plant. GM is a production oriented company and this emphasis results in parts substitutions, procedure changes, and a certain degree of inconsistency in all its product lines. Although the Corvette production has a higher degree of hand work and attention, the amount of on-line substitutions and changes is as much or more than other lines on a quantity related basis.

Production line inconsistency is one reason that no text can ever be written to detail every step required to restore every Corvette ever made. A hundred books couldn't do it. What can be done is to scrutinize one state-of-the art restoration like the Burroughs-Ellefsen project and use what's been learned from it to go on to further heights of the art.

Engine

The degree to which an engine is restored can vary greatly. Therefore, the time and expense allocated to engine restoration is very wide. The reason is the combination of engine condition and intended future use.

At one extreme is the engine which hasn't been started in years and is locked up. If you purchased a Corvette in very poor condition or one that has been improperly stored for several years, such an engine is a possibility. You have nothing to rely on as to the engine's internal condition other than the memory and honesty of the previous owner. There is real risk involved, but the more a restorer knows about engines the less likely he is to be intimidated. He realizes that most engines can be salvaged and what appears to be serious problems often turn out to be minor.

At the other extreme is the case where the restorer knows the history of the engine well and knows it to be in good working order. Ideally, the car has been in the restorer's possession for years. He knows how it has been treated, its strengths, weaknesses, and quirks like a high speed miss or a slightly high operating temperature. If the car was used only occasionally, these types of ailments may not have justified immediate attention. But restoration time is time to bring the engine back to perfection. Maybe.

The maybe depends on what's intended for the Corvette. There are those who would argue that if someone is going through the trouble of restoring a Corvette, everything that shows wear or damage should be replaced. This is valid, but a car being restored for occasional use which has a history of running reliably, has good compression, and uses only moderate oil could be left alone internally. Or there is the middle ground compromise of disassembling the engine to the "short block" stage. Valves can be ground and accessible sludge accumulation removed.

Everyone's ideal would be an original engine with low miles that has been properly cared for. Chances are it will need nothing but a cleanup. Still, it's wise to pull the valve covers and pan gasket to check for cleanliness. You should also consider pulling off every part that has a gasket behind it to stop the inevitable leaks that come with age regardless of use.

A second ideal is a totally rebuilt engine. Unfortunately, "totally rebuilt" is one of those grossly misused phrases used by people advertising Corvettes. It scares knowledgeable enthusiasts and many would rather purchase a Corvette with an engine that has not been touched, even if it's filthy and has an obvious ailment. The engine is the heart and soul of every Corvette and there's something scary about envisioning some rank amateur throwing a bench full of parts together that look very strange to him with a screwdriver and crescent wrench.

Whether you do your own engine work or send it out depends on your own ability and desire. The best way to learn how an engine really functions is to completely rebuild one. A person can watch someone else for years, but it takes a "hands on" rebuild to really understand. If you are patient, mechanically inclined, and willing to invest in tools you may use just a few times, plunge in. Nothing is more satisfying than rebuilding a sick engine into a fine running jewel.

Engine work can also be entrusted to others, and this is what Dave Burroughs did. This obviously costs more and takes the engine out of the restorer's personal control. If someone else does your engine, be sure his reputation is solid. Check with other Corvette enthusiasts in your area. If you're in a club, check with other members. They'll know who is good in your area. Never look in the phone book and pick a rebuilder based on phone conversations and cost quotes.

Regardless of who does the inner engine rebuild, some preliminary steps should be done by the restorer. Before the engine comes out of the car, its condition should be carefully documented. A restorer who has used the car extensively will have done mental documentation, but this should be recorded. Make visual observations and specific tests such as compression, operating temperature, oil pressure, and idle smoothness. Check

Right: This photo of the unrestored engine clearly shows that the area behind the exhaust manifolds was not painted. This means that the manifold was in place when the engine was painted. The pencil is pointing to the handwritten "I" which is short for "IF," the correct suffix designation for this 396 cubic inch, 425 horsepower engine.

Left: Paint patterns on the unrestored engine show that the water pump was on the engine when painted since the area behind the pump is unpainted.

Above and Right: Closer views of the area behind the water pump show that the timing case cover has likely never been removed. The top bolt heads are painted but the lower ones have little or no coverage. The coverage on the individual heads also indicates spraying from above. Another clue that the bolts have never been removed is that the paint on each is unscarred.

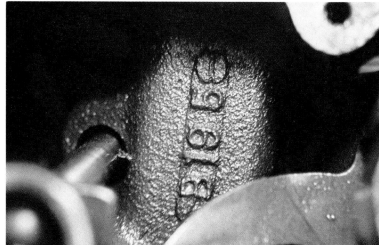

Much verification can be done by removing the valve covers and checking head markings. ''Hi Perf'' at left means this head is for a high performance engine. ''B195'' above means this head was cast on February 19, 1965, a date that should obviously precede the date the car was assembled. The seven digit code above is the GM casting number for this style head. Heads are not keyed to each Corvette but if all numbers are correct, there is little doubt about authenticity.

the exhaust pipe. A black or blue sooty appearance can mean an oil burner, but it can also be a carburetor mixture problem or poor valve seals. The exhaust pipe should be grey. If it isn't, that's just one more fact to document.

If compression tests indicate a low cylinder, pay special attention to that cylinder when the engine comes apart. Listen to the engine run. Does it run smoothly or does it surge? Is the noise level between cylinders even or is there a distinct valve train tick that may indicate a sticky lifter or worse? Any obvious problem will be corrected when the engine is rebuilt, but it helps greatly to have an idea where known problems are rather than assuming everything will be caught in the rebuild.

All of these things illustrate the importance of documenting the engine before teardown. But what if the engine is frozen or hasn't run in so long you're reluctant to turn it over?

Your reluctance is well founded. When you hear something like "She'd been in storage for fifteen years and all we did was pour some gas in the carb and hook up the battery . . . it took right off," you can be sure the guy is himself running on less than all eight. The danger in turning an engine over that hasn't run in a long time is that serious damage can result. Over a period of time, oil tends to drain off critical parts like the cylinder walls, bearing

Left: This is the block casting number. It's located at the upper rear of the block at the parting surface of the bell housing on the driver side.
Above: This is the engine casting date located on the lower side of the block next to the antifreeze plug on the passenger side. The "C-16-5" means the engine was cast on March 16, 1965. Don't be confused by the marks to either side of the code. These are left by screws that hold the changeable date code in the mold.
Right: The most well known engine numbers are these, located on a machined pad just forward of the passenger side head. The lower number is stamped when the engine is assembled and is a date, plant, and engine type code. T0329IF translates to a high performance 396 (IF), built at the Tonawanda, New York, plant (T), on the 29th of March (0329). The upper number is stamped in just before the engine is installed into the chassis. The last six digits correspond to the last six digits of the vehicle serial number. The 5 denotes the 1965 model year.

surfaces, and valve train. It's unlikely that the engine's interior surfaces will be laden with rust because the sealed nature of the engine tends to create an oil "atmosphere" that is quite protective. But some corrosion can take place that locks in a piston ring or bearing surface. Turning the engine over without first attempting to force some lubricant into these surfaces could result in a cracked ring, a gauled bearing, a sprung camshaft, or worse.

There is no failsafe method of insuring the introduction of lubricant into all critical areas of an engine that hasn't run in some

time. The accepted technique is to first pour a liberal amount of penetrating oil into all cylinders through the spark plug holes. Let it soak in for hours or even days, and repeat the procedure several times. Remove the valve covers and inspect the valve train. If you see evidence of rust, it's possible the valves could be rusted in the guides. You can drench everything in oil, or you could just take the head off and take it to your favorite auto machine shop for a valve job. Whether you remove the heads or not, try to turn the engine over by hand after it's had the penetrating oil treatment. If this doesn't work and the heads are off, try tapping the top of the pistons (except any in top or bottom dead center) with a wooden hammer. That should free a stuck ring.

After a stuck engine has been freed by the penetrating oil soak, don't try to start it until the oil has been changed. Penetrating oil is great for freeing up parts but not much of a lubricant. To play it extra safe, turn the engine over with the battery for a minute or two without starting, then change the oil again to minimize any chance of oil dilution.

Once the lubrication is taken care of the engine can be started. If it's reluctant to start, make the usual checks of fuel to the carburetor and fire to the spark plugs. If these check out, the plugs may be fouled by the oil you've been dumping on top of the cylinders. Try cleaning them.

Some restorers like to use one of the "quick start" products available to help a long silent engine get going. This stuff is extremely flammable. Be sure to replace the air cleaner cover because a backfire through the carb in the presence of a hot start compound can start a dandy blaze.

Once the engine is running, you may find that it idles but has little response. This could probably be due to a faulty accelerator pump in the carburetor. And don't be surprised if the carburetor leaks like a sieve. That's to be expected from dried out gaskets. Holly carburetors have a tendency to leak at the metering plate which may be distorted and require replacement or double-gasketing. The leaks likely to be encountered when restarting a long silent engine are ample reason to keep a fire extinguisher handy.

It is likely that the carburetor will be rebuilt, so to avoid the problems just discussed, you could just rebuild the carburetor

Above: The engine has been in and out of the test chassis several times and has now been debugged and is performing perfectly.
Below: Detailing begins with careful cleaning. The aluminum intake manifold is painted on many small block Corvette engines, but this is not the case with the 1965 big blocks. The manifold was just cleaned by hand. No glass beading or other material removal process was used. For stubborn stains, paint stripper can be effective.

Above: Cleaning continues. Note that the water pump and exhaust manifolds have been installed over unpainted areas.
Below: The rear of the engine has been masked since the factory painted it with bell housing in place. The intake manifold is masked, but loosely. Some completely original Corvettes have been observed with so much orange overspray on the intake manifolds, there's some doubt they were masked at all.

Above: The looseness of the intake manifold masking is clear, as are the correct valve cover retainers, exposed valve cover gasket edges, and exposed hose connecting the intake manifold to the water pump.
Below: Finished engine displays painted exhaust manifolds (yes, the paint will discolor and burn off). The pulley attached to the harmonic balancer should not be painted. This pulley was installed later at the assembly plant, as were the motor mounts and starter.

before attempting to start the engine. The nuances of carburetor rebuilding won't be detailed here, as it's a matter of carefully following the instructions packed with the rebuild kit. A fresh carburetor is a great investment for any Corvette and costs are minimal. But there are many parts in a rebuild kit and you must exercise great caution if you're a novice.

The problem with the instructions packed with the kit is that they usually show a "typical" carburetor. In other words, the instructions cover several models. If you carelessly turn a partially disassembled unit over and a few little silver balls go bouncing around the garage floor, you'll have a devil of a time figuring out where they came from. And some of the adjustments can be confusing to someone who doesn't understand their function.

Take it easy and get help if you need it. Save every part of your original carb you're replacing and be sure the replacements are exactly the same. Because kits are often for several variations of a carburetor style, frequently there are more parts than actually needed. Holly carbs in proper working order are favorites among Corvette owners because any good speed shop has every possible part in stock. It's less convenient with a Carter or Rochester.

As part of his plan to learn as much as possible while restoring his '65, Dave Burroughs combined some of the options regarding engine rebuild. He pulled it himself, and disassembled everything but the block. His interest was in determining as much as he could about how the engine was painted and finished by GM. Of course, he wanted to document the correctness and originality of the 396 engine also. He and Dale Smith photographed about every square inch inside and out.

To sum up what he learned, Dave put it this way. "There is paint where you would not expect it. There isn't paint in places you would expect it." Unlike restorers, GM did not meticulously paint each component before assembling the engine. On the contrary, GM considers engine paint cosmetic. What doesn't show doesn't need paint. (That's not entirely true because there are some parts painted but not seen when the engine is installed.)

The engines are painted in a GM engine plant in a nearly complete state, usually while suspended from the top. What is accessible to the sprayer is painted, what isn't . . . isn't. Just as Mike Hanson had theorized back in 1978, it was clear in Dave's documentation that components such as the water pump, exhaust manifolds, and bell housing were in place when the engine was sprayed. When these items were removed, the raw block and unpainted back of the oil pan were exposed.

This would be apparent to anyone who has torn down an un-molested Corvette engine, but these sorts of things go unnoticed unless real effort is made to identify what a lack of paint means. In the past, restorers have tended to paint engine parts separately before reassembling the engine. It would have been nice of GM to do it that way, but they didn't. If your goal is the natural factory look, don't respray the engine until it has been reassembled.

GM isn't out to win any awards for quality paint application on engines. The intake manifold of Dave's '65 396 had orange over-spray on it, typical of all aluminum manifold big blocks. The small hose connecting the intake manifold with the water pump likewise got a dose of orange. You can't look at one car and assume that all were done the same way, but Dave verified the sloppiness by viewing other untouched cars and studying original GM photos.

Subtleties like angle, thickness, texture, and location of paint overspray are the reasons that the real pros of the Corvette world often limit their range of interest to just a few models. Ask Dave Burroughs if some little gizmo on his '65 was oversprayed in the same direction on the '64 models and he may not know for sure. Ask him if it was the same way on early '65 models as it was on late ones and you'll probably get an answer. It may be something like "Well, I've viewed five 1965 models built during the first week of production and they were all like so. But the six late production models I've viewed were different. Of course, the factory assembly manual says there was a procedure change on February 12, 1965, which . . ." You get the point.

The other documentation Dave did as he disassembled the engine was to verify the correctness of the engine and its components. The block itself and many of the other engine parts are coded by GM and a knowledgeable restorer can decipher the codes to assure himself and others of the engine's originality. Like many automobile things, there are no absolutes here. You can't bet your life that because a head has the correct coding, it was the exact head which came with the car from the factory. What you can do is establish that parts are the correct type. If

Above: Inspection marks and coding are visible in this clutch photo. Also, "Hi Perf" (perf is visible) can be seen at the back of the block.
Right: Purchasers of early 396 "big block" Corvettes are often dismayed when they notice "pass" (passenger) cast into their block as shown in the upper left of this photo. The designation is confusing, but correct. Observe the degree of orange coverage on the exhaust manifolds which was typical of factory application. No overspray appears on the starter, exhaust pipe, or heat riser, as they were all installed after the engine was painted. The steel acorn nuts at the exhaust connections are correct, though many restorers change to brass.

everything corresponds correctly, you can be sure beyond a reasonable doubt that the block and its components are original. The opposite can be discovered as well.

Nice of GM to code these parts so we restorers could figure all this out later, right? Sorry, not the case. Most coding is done for the same reason the soup company puts those funny numbers on soup cans. If the janitor accidently dumps the trash into the chicken noodle crock, they need to be able to trace and remove the defective product. Similarily, GM needs to be able to pull defective parts from inventory stock before they get installed in automobiles. This holds true for the numbers that change daily such as date codes on castings. Other codes, such as the engine casting number on the back of blocks are consistent for a family of blocks

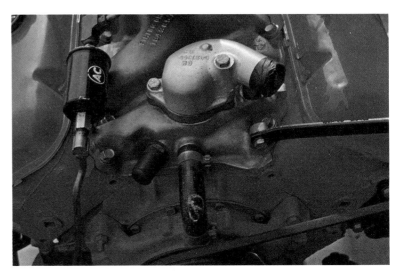

Left: This "after" restoration view gives a good feel for the correct degree of cosmetics a "natural factory look" restoration should have. The fuel filter is original and untouched. The lower connection into the water pump was unpainted. The intake manifold is oversprayed as it should be, but the serial number pad (see closeup on page 71) was masked or wiped clean.

Above: The end of the thermostat housing is shown masked where the hose will connect, but it's not certain the factory bothered. The housing itself should be painted silver, the spacer and the manifold are aluminum, resulting in different gradations of metallic silver.

Right: The Holley carburetor was added by the factory after the application of orange, so no overspray should appear on it. However, a trace of orange on the studs to which the carburetor mounts is correct and commonly seen on original cars.

and not constantly changed. And there are the previously discussed numbers necessary for later identification in theft recoveries.

When the engine for the Burroughs-Ellefsen restoration was returned by Jim Otto, the rebuilder, Dave wanted to test it to be sure it was functioning properly. He didn't want to put it back into the original chassis and risk scratches if it had to come back out. Dave had a spare 396 Corvette around so he used it as a test bed for the rebuilt engine. In this way, he could not only start the engine, but he could get it out on the road and test drive it. Yet the finished original chassis would not have seen a bit of road use.

These overall views portray how state-of-the-art restoration all comes together before the body drop. Note the subtle differences in black gloss in chassis components, the codes and markings, and the general lack of a ''just redone'' look. This is what is meant by a ''natural factory look'' restoration.

Dave's caution paid off. It was evident that something was definitely wrong with the engine the instant it fired. Back out it came. Back apart it came. It turned out to be a collapsed piston. Ultimately, Dave and Jim replaced all the pistons with new ones. In retrospect, Dave feels he should have taken Jim's advice and done this in the first place.

Engine problems are something some restorers would have a tendency to hide, even if they completely corrected them. Dave's philosophy is that if something didn't work, make history out of it. Figure out why it didn't work, fix it, then lay it out in documentation for everyone to see.

Dave had the engine in and out of the test car five times over the course of tests, re-tests, restoring and final detailing. He carefully recorded each test's results. On each run he documented the date, how far the car was driven, the length of time the engine ran, ambient air temperature, how much fuel was used, oil pressure characteristics, etc. This is all an outgrowth of Dave's other pas-

sion, airplanes. As a pilot, he's trained to log every detail of flight. This carried over to his documentation of the Corvette engine tests. This is despite the fact that the finished restoration will probably never be driven more than on and off a trailer. In fact, he and Don Ellefsen may decide to pickle the engine and never start it again. All this testing trouble for an engine that may never be used again? Yes.

A future owner of this car has every right to know just exactly what he has with no mysteries. So even though the chassis will have zero miles, the engine has gone through a complete 9.6 hour road course shakedown and all results carefully documented. A little extreme, you say? This is an extremely valuable automobile with three years and much capital invested. It deserved it.

We all don't have the luxury of a spare Corvette sitting around to use as a test bed for our engine. So how does all this relate? Depends on your goals and your restoration plan.

If you want to put a tested engine into your finished chassis, you can accomplish it a number of ways. One way would be to do (or have done) all engine work before even pulling the body. In this way, you could re-install the engine and drive the car to your satisfaction. Then the engine could come out, go into storage, and the rest of the restoration commence. This has the disadvantage of introducing a potential high cash outlay very early in the project.

Another idea would be to remove the body and work on it, but leave the chassis alone until the rebuilt engine could be installed and tested. You could rig the engine and listen to it run, but couldn't actually drive the chassis without a lot of additional rigging, or dropping the body back on.

The whole discussion is unnecessary if you're willing to gamble on dropping the finished engine into the chassis without prior testing. If your car is familiar to you, the gamble might not be great. The worst that would happen is that you just take it back out again. If your finished goal is considerably less than Dave's, the price of a mistake won't be that high.

Stage Four: Assembly

The joy of restoring a Corvette really starts to materialize when the final assembly starts. Sequenced correctly, all the components are ready to put back on or in the car and assembly goes very quickly. Up to this time hundreds of hours have been invested, often in parts that are just parts. There's pleasure in seeing the body finish completed, but nothing compares to the feeling the restorer gets as the assembly stage proceeds. There will be a few last minute hitches, but in a matter of days the car is virtually complete. People who run long distances tell of a "high" they sustain after six or seven miles are under their belt. And they say it's a feeling that only someone who's experienced it can imagine. Perhaps the same is true of the feeling a restorer gets when a year or two project comes together the last few days. It is indescribable.

Assembly is the easiest of the restoration tasks. Done properly, the earlier stages of disassembly and restoration with constant documentation and research are the phases that take the time. In the assembly phase, it all comes together. This is when the restorer's blood starts pumping as an automotive masterpiece, restored to show room condition, takes shape.

While it sounds simplistic, assembly is nothing more than reversing the disassembly process. And there is a tool available to Corvette restorers which, when followed correctly, will virtually assure proper factory reassembly.

The tool is called the factory assembly manual. There is a separate Corvette assembly manual for each Corvette model year (though not all are available). They were developed by GM engineers to show assembly plant personnel how to put the Corvette together. The detail is complete, right down to the last washer and screw. You have to root and search for what you want, but it's all there.

The factory assembly manuals were not developed by GM for sale to the public. But the value to Corvette restorers was so apparent that it was just a matter of time before someone made them available. Mid America Corvette Parts in Effingham, Illinois, led the way in reproducing the manuals for sale to enthusiasts, and many clones of the originals are now on the market.

If an assembly manual is available for the model year Corvette you're restoring, buy it. It'll pay for itself many times over.

Armed with an assembly manual and a well-documented disassembly, you're ready to begin the assembly process. Since it is virtually impossible for a restorer to duplicate exactly the assembly steps GM used, there is no single set of steps that must be followed. However, there are definitely sequence mistakes that can be made and the assembly manual won't help a bit in this regard. As a general guideline, the steps that Dave followed successfully in his restoration will be highlighted.

Complete the chassis. The engine, transmission, and suspension should all be installed, but do not install the water pump. The fuel tank should be in place with its rubber filler neck seal. The exhaust system should be completely installed except for the rear tips.

One of the things that Dave had pre-planned for the assembly stage was that the finished chassis and finished body would come together just once, just like at the factory. He didn't want to put the body on and off several times, and he wanted a minimum of work left after the two were united.

With these thoughts in mind, Dave decided to align the chassis without the body on. The factory does it that way, but it's a nightmare for a restorer without all the exotic apparatus the factory employs. A review of alignment principles here is necessary to understand how and why Dave went about this.

Over the past several decades, the vast majority of automobiles built in this country have been front engine, rear drive with solid rear axles. Corvettes built through the 1962 model are all of this configuration.

Starting in 1963, Corvettes became independently sprung at all four wheels. Compared to exotic or other sportscars, there was

Above: Dave Burroughs wanted to install the body on a completely finished chassis, including alignment. The factory does it this way, but uses rather exotic equipment to ''load'' the chassis to finished weight without the body. Dave accomplished the same thing with the assistance of other enthusiasts as they devised this simple but effective loading mechanism.
Right: Often ignored, the alignment of the Corvette's independent rear suspension is critical to correct handling and tire wear.

nothing revolutionary about this. But relative to what the average guy in an alignment shop in this country was used to seeing, this was strange.

In the typical American car of the past, only the front end had to be aligned. It was aligned for caster, camber, and toe-in. Of these terms, caster is the most difficult to understand. It is the amount of tilt about a theoretical vertical line through the center of the wheel of the front suspension. If you walk around to the front of your car and squat so that you're looking squarely at the tire tread, the amount that the tire leans in or out is measured by camber. Toe-in means that the distance between two opposing tires (say left front and right front) at the front tip is less than at the rear tip.

To someone who hasn't spent a great deal of time thinking about it, the idea of positioning wheels in anything but a perfectly straight up and down, no tilt attitude seems a might strange. It would appear that this would cause lousy tire wear. Well, it is true that a tire not running squarely to the road will not wear correctly. The problem is that if you set wheels when the car is in a static position, forces change the position when the car is moving. Different weights, steering geometry, and some trade-offs between steering effort and handling influence the engineers when they determine what ''correct'' settings should be. Understand that ''correct'' is a compromise.

Needless to say, if alignment settings are not correct, poor handling and poor tire wear result. If there's any one thing Corvette enthusiasts demand from their cars it is handling equal to the Corvette's capabilities.

The technique of aligning the Corvette's front end, that of shims between the upper ''A'' arm and a rigid frame member, is common to many American autos. But the rear is quite unique and for this reason countless Corvettes are on highways today with incorrect rear alignment. Even the most casual observer has noted Corvettes going down the street with the rear tires squatting out, maybe each tire squatting a different amount.

There is no caster alignment for the rear of Corvettes. The camber is set by adjusting an eccentric cam and bolt assembly

located at the inboard mounting of the strut rods. No shimming is required or possible. The toe-in (actually toe-out) adjustment is often ignored. It is done by slipping shims inside the frame member on both sides of the torque control arm pivot bushing. This isn't easy . . . maybe that's why it's ignored.

Dave Burroughs wanted all alignment out of the way before the body was lowered back onto the chassis. In terms of access, this is a great idea. There's only one problem. Without the weight of the body, the alignment settings will be wrong. But Dave was adamant and with the help of two Corvette enthusiasts, Chuck Rossmann and Mike Ilyin, a way was found. An ingeniously simple one at that.

Dave measured the ground clearance of another big block convertible with correct tires. Then the chassis of the Burroughs-Ellefsen '65 was "loaded" to the correct ground clearance with the use of chains and jacks on an overhead rack. You'll go crazy trying to talk your local alignment shop guys into a Rube Goldberg arrangement like this, unless they happen to be Corvette enthusiasts, too.

For most restorers, the technique Dave and his friends cooked up to align a chassis without the body on would make no practical sense. But there is a lesson to be learned here. Some people get things in their minds and they don't rest easily until they accomplish what they set out to do. There is very little that cannot be done with a little ingenuity, creativity, and imagination. These are the sort of challenges that restorers thrive on.

One of the last things to happen to the chassis of a mid-year Corvette before the body was dropped on at St. Louis was the factory black-out. This was no more than a quick shot of black paint on certain chassis components. Although the black-out had some cosmetic appeal, its main purpose was to prevent corrosion on visible components before the customer even took delivery. Nice as the idea was, it was typically done in a haphazard manner and GM no longer even bothers with it. But it was done at assembly to the Burroughs-Ellefsen '65 and Dave decided to duplicate it.

Dave observed as many similar models as possible to determine just how this black-out was applied. It wasn't very consistent. Dave noted that on some cars the black-out was fairly complete,

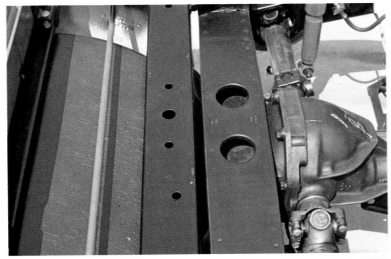

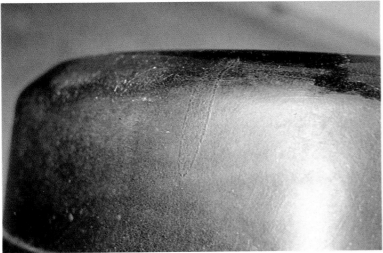

Above: The black-out operation typically caught part of the mufflers, sway bar, and a portion of the spare tire carrier. This photo also illustrates the gloss difference between the frame cross member and the differential carrier.
Below: This is the spare tire carrier during initial cleaning when it was discovered that parts of it were hit with black-out paint. Some of it was actually cleaned off, but some remains at the top of the carrier.

yet on others there was just a stripe on the mufflers and hardly anything on the half-shafts at all. It was clear that the painter just leaned over the chassis and gave the area a couple of quick shots. On Dave's '65, just one side of the half-shafts were coated. The painter obviously shot what was handy and didn't bother to lean under. Perhaps the workplace layout made it difficult. Whatever the reason, Dave simply tried to place himself back in the assembly plant environment. He didn't try to make the black-out perfect and he didn't take any special care to guard against overspray. With the chassis on the garage floor, he loaded up the spray gun, positioned himself where the factory painter would have been, then started spraying. Did it come out a little ragged? Sure, just as you would expect a '65 resting on a dealer's showroom in 1965 would have looked.

Satisfied with the black-out, Dave taped the shims in place and then removed the wheels, lowering the chassis onto wood blocks. Dave prefers having the chassis as low as possible when removing or replacing the body so that the height the body has to be lifted is minimized.

Prepare the body. Dave prefers not to have the hood on the body when it is put back on the chassis. Also, he wants it as light as possible, so he doesn't install interior components, glass, or trim. At the factory, just about everything was complete except for the seats, but this adds so much weight that it just isn't practical for the restorer to consider. The rear filler panel which surrounds the rear exhaust tips (in models without side exhausts) should also be left off until after the body drop.

One thing that shouldn't be left off is the throttle lever hookup that connects to the foot feed inside the car. This is very simple to do with the body removed, but the bell housing gets in the way after the body is on the chassis and a very simple task becomes very difficult. Another thing that's easier to do with the body off is to staple the mud flaps (in the engine compartment over the upper "A" arms) in place.

Body drop. As before, have eight people enlisted to do this. The restorer should **not** be one of the eight. The restorer should direct, not lift. Pay special attention to the rear area of the body as it's being lowered back to the chassis. The area where the rear fender curls under is easy to scratch, and the rear shims are easy to

This view of the black-out operation from below shows coverage representative of factory application. Some enthusiasts maintain the black-out was to prevent corrosion with the cosmetic aspect secondary. Others feel just the opposite. Either way, the results were never perfect and the areas involved were soon covered with road dirt anyway.

knock loose, tape or no tape. With the body now in place, the body bolts can be torqued in.

At this point of assembly, Dave prefers to do the final rubbing of the exterior finish. It could also be done before the body drop, but there is always the possibility of scratches during the body drop.

Dave researched factory finishing techniques and duplicated them on his '65 body. This was a straightforward technique involving rubbing compound and polish. Factory finishes of the era were characteristically smooth and shiny, but waves in the fiberglass were evident. A close-up of the paint would reveal that it was not a gorgeous, block-sanded surface. Therefore, Dave avoided the special tricks and techniques to achieve a mirror finish and just did it the way the factory did, complete with orange peel and a few dirt specs.

Install hard trim. The following list is not inclusive, nor is it in the order St. Louis used because factory assembly was done before the body was on the chassis. But these are the steps in order that Dave went through:

- electrical wiring
- antenna
- wiper motor
- dash cluster
- brake and clutch assembly
- windshield
- headlight and parklight assemblies
- taillight assemblies
- door latch and lock mechanisms
- door handles
- vent window assemblies
- side windows and regulators
- exterior windshield trim
- steering column (don't tighten until after driven)
- grill
- bumper brackets and bumpers
- rear filler panel
- exhaust tips, emblems

Connections and hookups. Often some of these are done while hard trim is being installed, but the logic sequence makes more sense if they're left as a group.

- heater box
- radiator and shroud
- water pump and fan
- overflow tank
- coolant hoses
- lines (fuel, oil, brake to master cylinder)
- linkages (throttle, clutch, parking brake)
- wiring or electrical connections (distributor, coil, starter, temperature sending unit, wiper motor, heater motor, alternator, regulator, battery, horn relay, horns.)
- cables (speedometer, tachometer, body-to-frame hold down)
- install hood

Add fluids. Add oil, fuel, coolant, and brake fluid. All should be to the levels recommended by the manufacturer, but Dave limits gasoline to two gallons at this point.

Prestart. In this step Dave bleeds the brakes, checks the parking brake and adjusts as required, then conducts an electrical test of the following:

- headlights, parking lights, turning lights
- taillights, brakelights
- back-up lights (if equipped)
- parking brake light
- interior lights
- headlight, heater, and antenna motors
- horns

Start and run-in. With all systems go, it's time to start the engine. Dave uses no elaborate procedure, but he doesn't recommend priming the carburetor for fast start. It will take the fuel pump several seconds to bring fuel from the tank into the carb. This will allow oil pressure to build before the engine starts.

Dave let his engine run only long enough to convince him all was well. He checks for required oil pressure, smooth idle, crisp acceleration rev-ups, and no run-on after engine is shut down. While the engine is running, do check for leaks or any signs of trouble.

Oil mist engine compartment. This is another example of the supreme effort made in the Burroughs-Ellefsen restoration for the natural factory look and factory originality.

When the mid-year Corvettes were completed at the factory, a light mist coat of water-soluable oil was sprayed into the engine compartment. This was another technique used by the factory to prevent surface rust from starting before the customer took delivery. It was purely a temporary fix, and after a few weeks of normal driving the effect of the mist coat was gone. But this procedure gave a certain look to the engine compartment that would have been apparent upon close inspection either at the factory or on the showroom. So of course, Dave put it in.

Install interior and trim. At the equivalent point in the factory procedure, only the seats would remain to be installed. But Dave feels it is best to leave the entire interior to last. Why risk climbing in and out of a brand new or freshly restored interior during earlier steps? Leave it to the last and do it with extreme care. The order of installation by Dave was:

The last piece of trim is applied by Dave Burroughs.

- jute and carpet (3-M brand adhesive spray #08080 works great)
- kick panels
- console
- steering wheel
- inside windshield trim
- radio and speaker
- glove box
- convertible top (if applicable)
- sill plates
- door panels and knobs
- seats
- decals, window stickers, tags

If component restoration has been sequenced correctly, the assembly process really is nothing more than putting the parts back together and it does go very quickly. In the case of the Burroughs-Ellefsen restoration, just one thing remained . . . the presentation.

The Presentation

On a brisk November Sunday, Dave Burroughs and his wife Carol invited the Ellefsens, Don and Evelyn, to the Burroughs' home for the official presentation. Mike Antonick, the author of this text, was also invited.

This was no "slam, bang" presentation. Dave had decided to play this to the hilt and kept everybody in suspense. Carol served an excellent meal and the suspense began to build. Dave had the entire day scheduled just as he had scheduled the entire restoration. Though everyone was dying to see the finished Corvette, sneak previews were not in the plan.

The dinner conversation ranged from the Chicago police force to Japanese baths. Cars weren't mentioned. That waited until after dinner when Dave led his guests to the den for a slide presentation of the restoration.

The show was staggering, enhanced by Dave's talents as an effective, low-key showman. It wasn't just a few "before" shots followed by an "after" shot. The slide presentation lasted an hour. It compressed into sixty minutes a project that had consumed four thousand hours and spanned three years. More importantly, Dave detailed not only what was done, but **why** it was done. Tremendous pains had been taken to give this car the **natural factory look,** and the obvious wisdom of this approach was suitably underscored.

Dave primed his guests almost to the breaking point, tantalizing and teasing. Then everybody was led to the garage for the unveiling.

The Corvette was there, covered and positioned so that the full driver's side faced the coming viewing. In front of the car was a small table, a bottle of cooling champagne, and a small plaque. The inscription read:

1965 396 Corvette

Presented to

Don Ellefsen

". . . The way it was. Not the way

we wished it was."

Burroughs No. 1

Don Ellefsen pulled back the cover, and there it was . . . a magnificent example of Chevrolet's Corvette, vintage 1965. Though the emotion was so thick in that chilly garage it could have been cut with a serving knife, for a few moments, not a word was spoken.

Time has been compared to a flowing river. We are floating along on a leaf at the same speed as the water, so we do not notice the movement of the river. The most that can be hoped for is that the leaf will be washed ashore and time will stop. But there is no way the leaf can float upstream. Going back in time belongs strictly in the science fiction realm.

Until Dave Burroughs, that is. For a moment in that Illinois garage, each person was in another time. For Antonick, the time was 1965 and the place was Dusty Rhodes Chevrolet in Mt. Vernon, Ohio. The brand-new '65 silver Corvette on display was just a dream. A dream that he and thousands of others would have hocked their eye teeth for. *text continues on page 95*

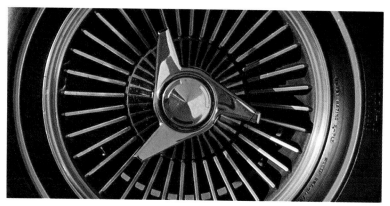

The emotions felt by the others during the brief silence are known only to them. Certainly pride was washing over the Burroughs . . . pride and perhaps relief washing over Dave for bringing the project to such a successful and meaningful conclusion, and Carol's pride in her husband's talents. There was joy in the eyes of the Ellefsens. They had come expecting no less than the best Corvette restoration ever done and they were sure they'd gotten it.

In case there has ever been any doubt, viewing the car in this manner made it abundantly clear why the mid-year Corvette was so successful when it was introduced, and why it only gains in stature as the years roll by. After the initial speechlessness, the chilly garage became a buzzing showroom.

This is a gorgeous and timeless automotive statement. It was gorgeous in 1965. It is gorgeous today. It will be gorgeous in 2025. This is a state-of-the-art automobile, the best of a period that will never be seen again. Preserving it demands no less than state-of-the-art restoration. It should be no less and no more than it was when it was built in 1965, because what it was . . . was perfect.

It is a classic, and with the proper restoration it can do the impossible. Not only can it stop a viewer cold, it can send the leaf upstream. It can, for an instant, turn back the calendar.

It is a time trip.

". . . The way it was.
Not the way we wished it was."

The Art of Fiberglass Repairs
From the Folks at Ecklers

No Corvette restoration book can be complete without a discussion of fiberglass repair techniques. This is a frightening subject to many would-be restorers, both from the standpoint of doing the work themselves, or finding someone they can trust to do it for them.

The fear is well founded. It is safe to say that many Corvettes have not been repaired properly. It shows. There's a general feeling that craftsmanship has all but departed from the body repair business, that modern shops employ people who are simply capable of removing damaged parts and bolting new ones on. That's fine for a metal car, but it's not so easy for fiberglass. It still takes skill and care to repair a fiberglass car properly.

The skills are not that difficult to master. Most enthusiasts willing to tackle a restoration are capable of mastering sufficient skills to handle all but major repairs.

Obviously, a key ingredient to success in fiberglass repair is to have the correct materials, along with state-of-the-art knowhow. Afterall, fiberglass is a relatively new material. The science of how to use it is constantly changing and improving. There are literally hundreds of fiberglass repair products on the market, so it appears the logical thing to do is to deal with someone who is aware of the latest technology and who specializes in Corvettes.

With this thought in mind, the publisher sought assistance from Ecklers, the world leader in Corvette fiberglass panels and repair products. The publisher acknowledges with appreciation the following article and photography which was provided by the staff of Ecklers for inclusion in this text.

Over the years, the repair of fiberglass bodies has been treated as a great mystery. Most owners of fiberglass bodied automobiles have left this type of work to "experts," fearing that any attempt at repair would surely have disastrous results.

In reality, repair of fiberglass bodies is no more or less difficult than that of steel bodies. With the proper materials, the novice and the experienced bodyman alike can produce excellent results.

The old image of the bodyman with rubber gloves, a coffee can full of "sticky stuff" and bits of fiberglass stuck all over himself is terribly misleading. Fiberglass repair need not be messy if proper methods are used.

Eckler's Corvette Parts has spent considerable time and effort on the research and development of fiberglass related materials which are durable, dependable, and which offer consistently superior results to the user.

There are no "secret" materials involved and all are available by mail through our sales division.

The materials referred to are listed below in order of use:

1. Eckler's Bonding Adhesive
2. Eckler's Resin
3. Eckler's Body Filler
4. Eckler's Spray Gelcoat

As is the case with any job involving craftsmanship, the quality of the finished products is often directly related to the tools that are used. Appropriate tools are referred to in the following text and shown in the accompanying photos.

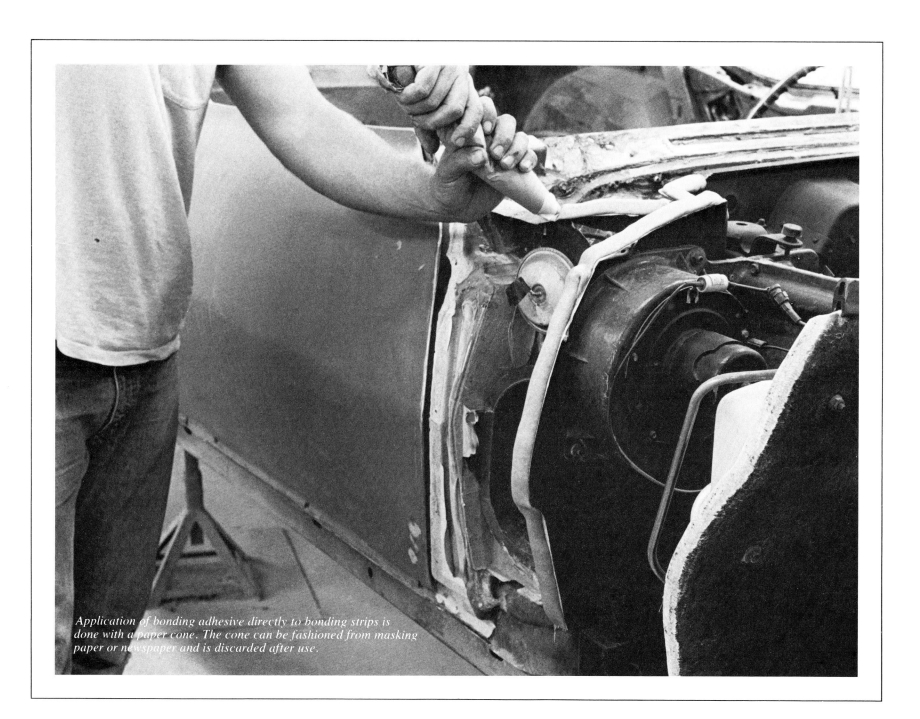

Application of bonding adhesive directly to bonding strips is done with a paper cone. The cone can be fashioned from masking paper or newspaper and is discarded after use.

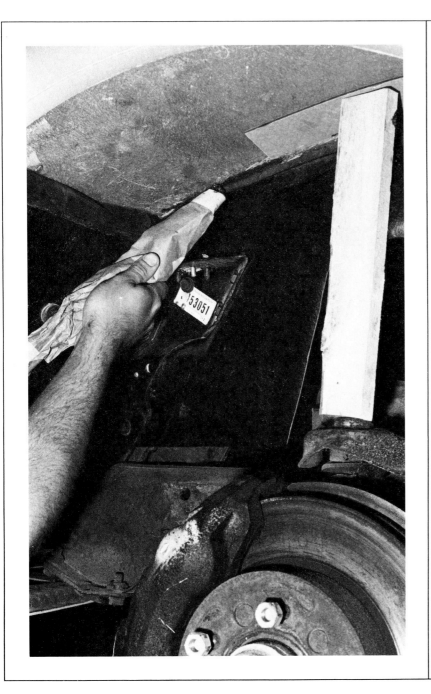

Bonding Adhesive

Eckler's bonding adhesive is a specially formulated polyester adhesive that is used for bonding fiberglass together.

It is very similar in appearance to body filler, but the chemical composition of these two materials is quite different. Bonding adhesive does not contain the same type of filler particles as body fillers and cannot be built up as heavily.

Bonding adhesive maintains some of its elasticity after curing. This gives it the ability to "grip" even in instances of severe expansion, contraction, and vibration. However, this elastic quality makes bonding adhesive difficult to sand and its porous composition does not readily accept painting. As a general rule, bonding adhesive and body filler should never be substituted for each other.

Fiberglass cannot be successfully edge glued and any joint or seam must be backed with a bonding strip. The Corvette body is manufactured in several sections which are then bonded to the body superstructure. Each of these sections is held in place by bonding strips. A bonding strip is a narrow strip of fiberglass (usually one to three inches wide) which conforms to the inside contour of the panels being bonded.

Before any bonding is attempted, all old adhesive must be ground away and new panels trial-fitted. Proper alignment of body panels is critical to the appearance of the finished job. Common procedure here is to carefully align the new panels and then drill and screw them into place. After any final adjustments are made, the panel is removed, bonding adhesive is applied to the bonding strips, and the panel is screwed back in place using the same holes. In this manner, final fit is certain and it is easier to repair the screw holes than to remove and re-bond a panel.

Before applying bonding adhesive, the bonding strips and the bonding areas on the inside of the new panel must be ground

Left: Factory panels occasionally "pop" loose. Bonding adhesive is the proper material to repair the area. The photo shows the inner fender area, a typical problem location.

thoroughly with a 24 or 36 grit disc. This leaves a sufficiently rough enough surface for the bonding adhesive to "grip" and also cleans away surface residue.

After grinding, all bonding areas should be wiped with a clean dry cloth and blown clean with compressed air. Solvents are not used for cleaning because they can soak into the raw fiberglass and affect the performance of the bonding adhesive.

Bonding adhesive can be easily and efficiently applied by using a paper cone in the same manner as a cake decorator would apply frosting to a birthday cake. Masking paper or newspaper is rolled into a cone shape and properly mixed bonding adhesive is dropped into it. The bonding adhesive can then be quickly and neatly squirted onto the bonding strips as needed with little or no mess.

Occasionally, factory installed body panels on a Corvette may pop loose. This is most common on front inner fender wells. When this condition occurs, the bonding areas should be spread gently apart and sanded between with 36 or 40 grit sandpaper. Then a paper cone, as just mentioned, is used to force bonding adhesive into the joint, the bonding areas are aligned, and adhesive is allowed to cure.

Resin and Fiberglass Mat

Eckler's Resin R-916 is another polyester based product. Although all polyester resins have similarities, Eckler's Resin is specially formulated for fast curing time and minimal shrinkage.

Resin is almost always used in conjunction with fiberglass cloth or mat. For repair purposes, mat works best. The random length and direction of the fibers gives it excellent strength and rigidity. Also, fiberglass mat is generally thicker than the woven cloth which gives it excellent build-up qualities.

Woven fiberglass cloth has acceptable resistance to tearing and is very flexible, but its woven pattern will eventually show through the finish material. We do not recommend its use.

Right: The special compounds available from Eckler's and discussed in this presentation are shown here. They include: Bonding Adhesive, Body Filler, Resin, and Spray Gelcoat.

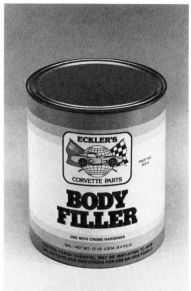

Above: Exterior body repair areas should be "dish ground" deep enough to allow the application of three layers of fiberglass mat with resin.
Below: After grinding, the residue is dusted with a cloth and blown clean with compressed air. Solvents shouldn't be used because they can soak into the raw fiberglass and affect later bonding.

Above: Three layers of fiberglass mat are applied and saturated with properly mixed resin. Eckler's doesn't recommend fiberglass cloth because the woven texture has a tendency to show through later. Note the masking of lower body panels.
Right: The resin-mat mixture is rolled. This serves the dual purpose of forcing out air bubbles and compressing the mixture for greater strength.

When splicing panels together or repairing severe fractures in fiberglass in an area where no bonding strip is present, the underside should be reinforced first. This is done by preparing the underside surface and applying two to three layers of fiberglass mat with resin. Repair work to the outside should not be attempted until the underside reinforcement has cured thoroughly.

If a bonding strip is present underneath a splice or fracture, or if the crack in question is merely superficial, no special attention to the underside is necessary (providing that all panels are bonded securely in place).

Any area being prepared for fiberglass application must first be ground with a 24 or 36 grit disc. This leaves a sufficiently rough enough surface for the resin to "grip".

If the repair work is being done on the outside of the body, the repair areas are "dish ground" (concave) deep enough to allow the application of three layers of fiberglass mat with resin. In the

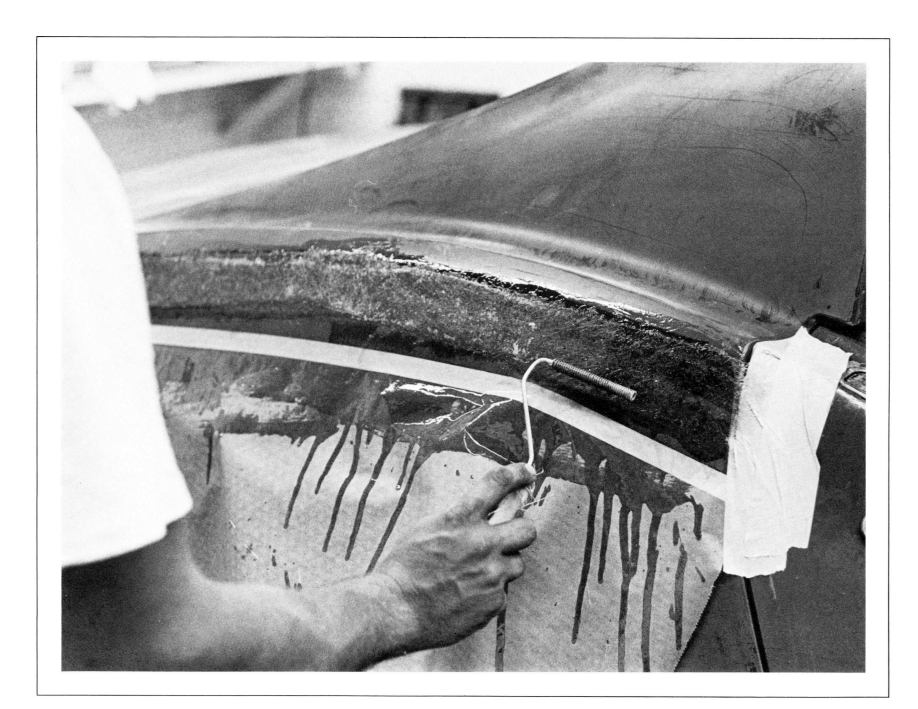

case of a splice or fracture, the center of the repair area is usually ground down to the bonding strip or reinforcement layer underneath.

After grinding, the repair areas are wiped with a clean dry cloth and blown clean with compressed air. Solvents are not used because they can soak into raw fiberglass and affect the new resin.

Surrounding areas are masked off to keep the resin from sticking where it shouldn't, and fiberglass mat is pre-cut to fit.

Polyester resin is mixed according to instructions on the can with MEKP hardener. Extreme care should be taken when handling MEKP hardener. It is a skin irritant and is extremely dangerous to the eyes. Wearing safety goggles is highly recommended when handling this substance.

Mix only enough resin to do the job at hand. Do not mix the whole can at once and do not put unused portions back in the can.

After mixing, a coat of resin is brushed onto the prepared areas and fiberglass mat is laid in place. The fiberglass mat is thoroughly saturated with resin and a second layer is applied immediately.

After the second layer is saturated, air bubbles and excess resin are rolled out. The third layer is applied immediately, saturated, and rolled again.

Rolling the fiberglass serves two purposes. It not only eliminates air bubbles and excess resin, but also helps to compress the glass fibers which adds strength.

Tools and utensils are cleaned immediately after use with acetone or lacquer thinner.

As soon as the resin has cured, masking is removed and the new fiberglass is ground down slightly below the desired finish contour in preparation for body filler.

Body Filler

Body filler is a controversial subject. In addition to standard polyester body fillers there are body fillers with glass beads added, body fillers with plastic beads added, body fillers with glass fibers added, and a number of other "miracle" concoctions. Ask any ten experienced bodymen which is best and you'll get ten different answers.

Above: Once the resin-mat mixture has cured, masking is removed and the repair is ground down slightly below the desired finish contour.
Right: The repair is again wiped and blown clean, then body filler is applied. This filler will only stick to raw fiberglass (or metal) and should not be applied over paints or primers.

With this in mind, Eckler's set about the task of finding the best type of body filler for use in fiberglass repair.

After extensive experimentation, a formula was found which provides excellent adhesion, applies smoothly, and has virtually no shrinkage. Although Eckler's body filler was formulated primarily with fiberglass repair in mind, it works equally well on steel.

Before body filler is applied, the repair area must be ground clean using a 24 or 36 grit disc. The area is then wiped with a clean dry cloth and blown clean with compressed air. Again, no solvents are used because they can be absorbed by raw fiberglass and may cause problems with the body filler later.

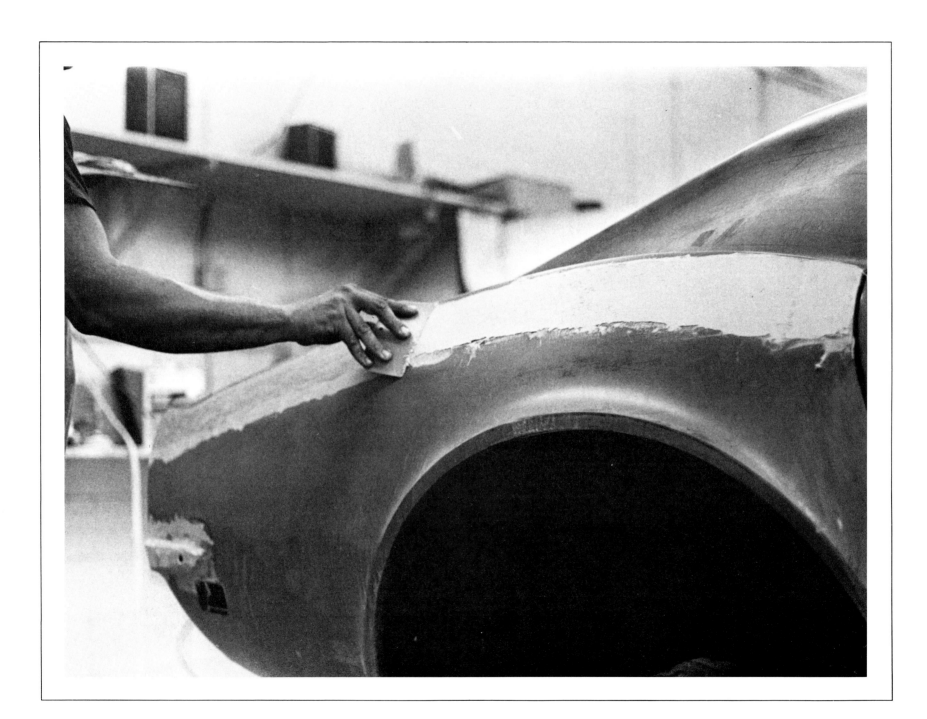

Left: The "cheese grater" file can be used to easily shape the repaired area to the approximate contour as soon as the fiberglass is rubbery.
Above: Only after the fiberglass has cured is it sanded to final contour with 40 and then 80 grit standpaper.
Right: If desired, the repair can be sprayed with gelcoat. This is a pure resin coating, applied with standard spray equipment (be sure to clean equipment right after use!) which duplicates the factory technique and helps prevent later bleed through. A mist coat is followed by four to six wet coats.

It should be stressed here that body filler is not intended to be applied over paint or primer. If all traces of these materials are not removed or ground away, the body filler will eventually lift and break out.

Body filler is applied (after mixing with hardener) to the prepared surface with a plastic paddle or squeegie. Obviously, the smoother it is applied, the less work will be required for finishing.

As soon as the body filler hardens to a rubbery stage, a "cheese grater" type body file is used to cut it to approximate correct contour. The body filler is then allowed to harden completely and 40 grit standpaper is used to achieve final contour. A sanding block is always used wherever possible.

Occasionally it may be necessary to make more than one application of body filler to an area in order to achieve the correct contour. If so, the above steps are merely repeated until the appropriate contour is attained.

After the correct contour is achieved, the entire area is block sanded with 80 grit sandpaper to remove the 40 grit sand scratches and any remaining grinder marks.

Spray Gelcoat

Eckler's Spray Gelcoat is a newcomer to the fiberglass repair products market. Spray gelcoat is another polyester-based product developed by Eckler's for use in several areas of Corvette body repair.

Corvette bodies are manufactured with a gelcoated surface. The purpose of gelcoat is to seal down the glass fibers in the substrate material and provide a durable and stable surface for finishing.

Eckler's Spray Gelcoat is a repair or replacement for the original gelcoat which has deteriorated or which has been damaged.

Surface checking or "crazing" which is evident on some older Corvettes is usually caused by deterioration of the original gelcoat. Simply sanding these minute cracks and loose fibers away

and repainting the surface will not eliminate the problem. The "crazing," checking, and loose fibers will reappear in a matter of weeks because the real cause of the problem has not been eliminated. Spray Gelcoat, if applied properly, will cure this problem indefinitely.

Stress cracking is another common problem which arises with fiberglass. Stress cracks usually occur in areas which have been subjected to impact or severe flexing. Similar to the way that safety glass shatters, if fiberglass is bumped or forced to flex unnaturally, it will send hairline cracks out in all directions. These cracks or "runners" may not be immediately visible, but will eventually show through as hairline cracks in the paint.

Severe cracks or fractures must be ground out and repaired with fiberglass mat and resin. Most other stress cracks, providing they are not in areas of continued flexing or stress, may be eliminated by the application of spray gelcoat.

Spray gelcoat will also eliminate bleed-through of resin or body filler in areas that have been repaired. Spray gelcoat must be applied over bare fiberglass, body filler or other gelcoat. It will not stick to paint, primer or metal surfaces.

The surface being gelcoated must first be sanded thoroughly with 80 grit sandpaper. This gives a sufficiently rough surface for the spray gelcoat to "grip."

Surrounding areas are masked off to keep the spray gelcoat from going where it's not wanted. Then all repair areas are wiped down with enamel reducer and dried with a clean cloth.

Spray gelcoat and MEKP hardener are mixed according to the instructions on the can and loaded into an ordinary siphon-feed spray gun. Additional expensive equipment, such as airless sprayers or pressure pots, are not needed.

A light mist coat is applied to all repair areas first. The mist coat is followed immediately by four to six heavy wet coats. Masking is removed immediately and the fresh gelcoat is allowed to cure overnight.

Left: The cured gelcoat is sprayed with a contrasting color of lacquer to aid in finding rough spots, then worked smooth with 80 grit sandpaper. Sand until all traces of lacquer are gone. Then respray a light coat of lacquer and resand with 220 grit sandpaper wet. The repair is now ready to prime.

Spray equipment is cleaned immediately after use with acetone or lacquer thinner because spray gelcoat will harden in the gun!

After curing, a mist coat of lacquer paint in a contrasting color is sprayed over the gelcoat. This is to aid in finding rough spots during sanding.

The entire area is block sanded with 80 grit sandpaper. Edges of the new gelcoat must be feather edged carefully. When all traces of the paint are gone, the gelcoat should be smooth.

After sanding with 80 grit sandpaper, the gelcoated areas are mist painted again and block sanded wet with 220 grit sandpaper.

If the gelcoat is sanded through, it must be roughed up with 80 grit again and spotted in with more spray gelcoat.

As soon as wet sanding is completed, the repair areas are washed down with enamel reducer again and wiped dry with a clean cloth. Primer can be applied in the normal fashion and prepared for finishing.

A rule of rule of thumb when making fiberglass repairs is that the various materials should be used for the specific purposes for which they were designed. A great deal of experimentation and testing has gone into the development of Eckler's products. Consistent results and dependable performance can be assured only if these materials are used properly.

Good luck!

Credits

- The 1965 feature Corvette is owned by Don Ellefsen and was restored by Dave Burroughs. Technical research for the restoration was provided by Cliff Gottlob, Mike Hanson, Jim Krughoff, and H.C. Schneider. Technical specialists were Jack Brandt, Greg Brinkman, Jim Heyungs, Hughes Engineering, Mike Ilyin, Dr. Bill Miller, Jim Otto, Chuck Rossmann, Royal Coach Ltd., and Dale Smith. Transportation was arranged by Harold Burroughs, Allan Vogelsang, and Ron Anschuetz. Special thanks to Bloomington Battery and Strickland Chevrolet for parts assistance, and to Carol Burroughs and Evelyn Ellefsen for patience and understanding.
- The text through page 97 was written by Mike Antonick with the assistance of Dave Burroughs. The fiberglass repair section on pages 98 through 109 was provided by Eckler's Fiberglass Division, PO Box 5637, Titusville, Florida, 32780.

● John Amgwert photographed or provided the photos appearing on pages 5, 7, and 18. The Corvette appearing on page 5 is from the Amgwert collection. The photo on page 11 was provided by Bill Locke. General Motors Photographic provided the photos on page 22. Corvette-Porsche comparison data is used courtesy of Road & Track Magazine. The classic '57 Corvette ad appearing on page 19 is from the collection of Carl Strohm and reprinted courtesy of the General Motors Corporation. All photographs of the Burroughs-Ellefsen 1965 Corvette are by Dale Smith and Gary Steiner. Photos appearing on pages 98 through 109 were provided by Eckler's Fiberglass Division.

● Graphic design is by Mike Antonick. Illustrations appearing on pages 8, 12, 15, 17, and 21 are by Dick Yoakam. Cover design by Mike Antonick and Dick Yoakam.